# ROUTLEDGE LIBRARY EDITIONS: TRANSPORT ECONOMICS

Volume 18

# RAILWAY ECONOMICS

# RAILWAY ECONOMICS

## K.G. FENELON

Routledge
Taylor & Francis Group

LONDON AND NEW YORK

First published in 1932 by Methuen & Co Ltd

This edition first published in 2017
by Routledge
2 Park Square, Milton Park, Abingdon, Oxon OX14 4RN

and by Routledge
711 Third Avenue, New York, NY 10017

*Routledge is an imprint of the Taylor & Francis Group, an informa business*

© 1932 Methuen & Co Ltd

*British Library Cataloguing in Publication Data*
A catalogue record for this book is available from the British Library

ISBN: 978-0-415-78484-9 (Set)
ISBN: 978-1-315-20175-7 (Set) (ebk)
ISBN: 978-1-138-63739-9 (Volume 18) (hbk)
ISBN: 978-1-138-63683-5 (Volume 18) (pbk)
ISBN: 978-1-315-20546-5 (Volume 18) (ebk)

**Publisher's Note**
The publisher has gone to great lengths to ensure the quality of this reprint but points out that some imperfections in the original copies may be apparent.

**Disclaimer**
The publisher has made every effort to trace copyright holders and would welcome correspondence from those they have been unable to trace.

# RAILWAY ECONOMICS

BY

K. G. FENELON, M.A., Ph.D.

METHUEN & CO. LTD.
36 ESSEX STREET W.C.
LONDON

*First Published in 1932*

PRINTED IN GREAT BRITAIN

# JOSEPH SHIELD NICHOLSON

M.A., SC.D., LL.D., F.B.A.

Late Professor of Political Economy in the University of
Edinburgh

' The Roman roads, straight over the hills, and their
bridges over great rivers, were in their day marvels of
construction; but they cannot be ranked with the railways
that are tunnelled through mountains and carried over
great arms of the sea. . . . Transport and communications
by land and water, the basis of industrial organization,
during the present century have revolutionized the
world, and we have already ceased to wonder at powers
which former ages could not even imagine as attributes
of their deities.'—J. S. NICHOLSON, *Principles of Political
Economy*, Vol. III, Book IV, pp. 21-2.

# PREFACE

BRITISH railways have had their full share of the economic difficulties of the post-war period. General industrial depression and changes in the direction of trade have had adverse reactions on railway finance; the rapid rise of road transport competition has largely transformed the economic conditions of pre-war days, so that railways no longer enjoy the same measure of monopoly; the provisions of the 1921 Act in regard to grouping have involved the companies in a complete re-organization of their systems, while the same Act has been responsible for elaborate statutory alterations in the structure of their tariffs; the growth of labour organization has revolutionized industrial relationships between the companies and their employees, and has led to considerable modification in wages, hours, and conditions of service; finally, technological progress has proceeded at a rapid pace and has necessitated many changes in operating technique and equipment. It therefore seems opportune to attempt a re-examination of the whole field of railway economics in the light of present-day conditions.

The railways, with their various ancillary enterprises, must be regarded as a whole, and on this account some attention is devoted in this book to questions of road transport services and railway-owned docks. In view of the public attention which has been focussed on certain aspects of railway working by the Reports of the Royal Commission on Transport and the Weir Committee on Main Line Electrification, it has seemed advisable to discuss in some detail the problems of railway electrification and the economics of train working. The main aim of the author, however, has been to provide a survey of railway economics as a whole, including railway labour, capital, organization, and administration; statutory regulations; amalgamation;

vii

the Railways Act 1921; and the theory and practice of railway charging.

To a certain extent, parts of the book are based on various courses of lectures delivered by the author during the past ten years in the Universities of Edinburgh and St. Andrews. He therefore hopes that the book may be found not unsuitable to the needs of railway students as well as to the requirements of the wider public interested in the problems of our railways. Since, however, railway economics impinges on the whole range of economic theory, railway students are advised to study some good text-book on general economics in conjunction with this work. Students are also recommended to keep in touch with new developments by reading some of the excellent technical publications now available, such as the *Railway Gazette* and *Modern Transport.*

Where possible the author has attempted to acknowledge his indebtedness to other writers by references in the footnotes and the bibliography. In particular, however, he desires to record his debt to the standard works of Acworth, Hadley, Colson, and Sherrington.

The author's grateful thanks are due to Professor A. Gray of Aberdeen University, who encouraged him to write the book and who made numerous suggestions for its improvement. For assistance in obtaining material and information he is indebted to Mr. J. Calder (General Manager, Scotland, L.N.E.R.); Mr. W. Wood (Electrical Engineer, Scotland, L.N.E.R.); Mr. G. S. Begg (Passenger Manager, S.S.A. L.N.E.R.); and Mr. A. Winter Gray (Secretary, Institute of Transport). He wishes also to thank especially Dr. Mary T. Rankin (Edinburgh University); Mr. James Fairlie (Rates and Fares Clerk, S.S.A. L.N.E.R.); and Mr. W. N. Kerr (General Manager's Office, Scotland, L.N.E.R.) for their valuable suggestions for the improvement of certain chapters.

K.G.F.

MANCHESTER,
*December*, 1931.

# CONTENTS

# RAILWAY ECONOMICS

## CHAPTER I

## INTRODUCTION

IN modern economic, social, and political organization the railways play a very important part, and it is largely as a result of the development of the railway that modern conditions have been evolved. All the characteristics of the modern industrial period—intensive division of labour, specialization of industry, large-scale production, localization of industry, the growth of great cities, world-wide markets, world supplies of raw materials—are dependent on adequate and efficient means of transport.

Transport gives to commodities the utility of being in the places where they are required, and thus it is to be classified in economic science as an essential stage in the production of wealth. It is often said that transport is non-productive, but this is fallacious. Transport enables raw materials to be brought into the economic conjuncture where they can be utilized to the best advantage, and it makes possible the placing of the finished product in the hands of the consumer, thus completing the work of production.

### THE DEMAND FOR RAILWAY TRANSPORT

The demand for transport arises from the fact that ' place values ' differ. This gives an economic incentive to the development of transport, so that commodities plentiful, or not required in one district, may be moved to other places where they are scarce or in demand.[1]   The distribution of some things, e.g. water or brick-clay, is almost universal, but that of others, such as wheat or cotton, is regionalized, while that of yet others, e.g. coal, potash, or diamonds, is restricted to certain localities.   These distinctive groups of commodities have been conveniently described by Alfred Weber as respectively ' ubiquities ', ' regional ubiquities ', and ' localized materials.'[2]

A commodity will be transported between two places, ' A ' and ' B ', if its cost of production in ' A ' plus the cost of transport to ' B ' is not greater than the cost of production of a similar article in ' B '.   If the cost of transport rises so that it only just pays to transport the commodity, the margin of transportability is reached, and if the transport rate were increased still further the commodity would no longer be transported, i.e. the rate would be higher than the traffic would bear.

F. W. Taussig points out in his *Principles of Economics* that ' ability to stand the transportation charge is the test of the utility of the carriage '.[3]   Subsidization of transport, therefore, is not economically justified unless there is a clear social gain to be obtained, such as diffusion of the population, or the economic development of a new country. Nevertheless in many countries, subsidies have been granted to various forms of transport, but in these cases political, military, or other non-economic advantages are held to outweigh the economic loss involved.

To traders and manufacturers, transportation charges are an important element in costs of production and therefore they have a considerable influence in determining the location of industries and factories, especially if the raw materials, or the finished products, are heavy, bulky, or otherwise expensive to carry.   Thus an industry using heavy raw materials, but producing commodities which

---

[1] The technical and engineering problems involved in the supply and location of railways will be found ably set forth in A. M. Wellington's *Economic Theory of the Location of Railways* (1887).
[2] *Theory of the Location of Industries*, pp. 50-1.
[3] Vol. II, p. 390.   (Third Edition.)

are considerably more valuable in proportion to weight, would be located at the source of the raw materials, while an industry utilizing 'ubiquities' as raw materials and of which the product is heavy would be decentralized, and factories would be set up near the various large towns.[4]

As the cost of transport is reduced, and as its efficiency becomes greater, other factors in location become of more importance. Improved transport thus furthers geographical division of labour, and unless trade is hindered by artificial barriers such as tariffs, it fosters the development of a world economy.

Also, as transport becomes cheaper, the radius of effective competition open to a trader is increased. This increased market competition is often very complex, since on the one hand the trader can tap new markets for the sale of his products, but on the other hand it may increase competition in his old markets. The effects are not always what might be expected; for example, Cliffe Leslie showed in 1872 that the construction of railways in Germany tended to increase the cost of living by raising local prices to a level with world prices.[5]

### THE DEMAND FOR PASSENGER TRANSPORT

The demand for passenger transport differs according to the purpose for which it is required. Some persons travel in connexion with their business, and to these transport

[4] Cf. Alfred Weber, *Theory of the Location of Industries.* See also Johann von Thünen, *The Isolated State* (published 1826). Von Thünen showed that in an isolated city surrounded by a fertile plain, bordered at its extremities by waste land, the location of agricultural pursuits and presumably industry would be determined by transportation costs, localization being effected in a series of concentric rings. Those zones nearest the town would be used in growing produce heavy in proportion to value or perishable commodities unsuited to transport over long distances.

[5] 'A much lower scale of the prices of land, labour, animal food, and other main elements of the cost of living to large classes, will usually be found to prevail in places without steam communication than in places similarly situated in other respects but possessing railways or steam transport by water.'—*Essays in Political and Moral Philosophy*, p. 331. (First Edition.)

is a *producers' utility*.  Increasing specialization of occupation and greater localization of industry, together with the
growing tendency of city populations to live outside the
central areas, have greatly intensified this form of the
demand for transport.  Other persons travel for pleasure,
or at least to reach pleasure resorts, and to these transport
is directly or indirectly a *consumers' utility*.  The intensity
and elasticity of the various types of demand varies, and
in order to attract holiday traffic the railway companies
have found it necessary to quote fares lower than those
applicable to ordinary travel.

During the past fifty years or so there has been a
cumulative rise in the demand for passenger transport and
the annual number of journeys per head of the population
has steadily increased, though during recent years motor
transport has absorbed a great part of this increase and
has taken some of the railway's old traffic.

Both as regards passenger and goods transport, the
demand is generally elastic, i.e. a decrease in the price of
transport leads to a considerable extension in the demand
for it.  This has been well illustrated by the remarkable
increase in third-class travel after 1872, when third-class
carriages were attached to practically all trains.  Demand
is said to be of unit elasticity if a fall in price is counter-
balanced by a corresponding extension in the amount sold,
so that receipts (i.e. price per unit multiplied by the
quantity sold at that price) remain constant.  It would
appear that up to a point the elasticity of demand for
rail transport is greater than unity, but after that point
it is less than unity.  The Passenger Manager and the
Goods Manager of a railway therefore have to obtain by
experiment the level of rates and fares which will afford
the greatest revenue.  If prices are fixed too high, the
gain will be below the maximum possible, and if too
low, the receipts will again be less.  In practice many
complications occur since the elasticity of different kinds
of traffic vary and only part of the working costs is fixed.
The remainder fluctuates with the traffic, being generally

less per unit of traffic as traffic increases, but sometimes greater, as when additional traffic involves the provision of another set of rails. However, the main point is that total costs are increased and therefore the responsiveness of demand to reductions in price would require to be so much the greater in order to cover the extra working costs involved. On the other hand a reduction in traffic, e.g. during a period of trade depression, might enable certain costs to be reduced because fewer trains are run, overtime is reduced, and casual labour is not required. During trade depression also economies may sometimes be obtained as a result of the reduced prices of materials.

Variations in the general price level have serious reactions on railway prosperity. If prices are rising, revenues tend to fall behind, since rates and fares cannot quickly be adjusted to the new level, while if prices are falling, wages and certain fixed charges cannot be reduced at the same rate.

### THE ELEMENTS INVOLVED IN RAIL TRANSPORT

In the provision of any form of transport, several distinct elements can be distinguished. These are: (1) the motive power, (2) the vehicle or vessel, (3) the roadway, and (4) the terminals, e.g. stations, docks, or air ports. Sometimes one or more of the elements may be provided free by nature, e.g. the highway of the air, or they may be provided free by the community, e.g. canalized rivers or bus stances. In other cases the elements may be provided by different sets of persons, e.g. on British canals, by-traders provide carriage. A canal rate is therefore composed of two elements: (1) a toll for the use of the waterway and (2) a charge for the special costs of transit.

When railways were first built, the promoters naturally thought that the practice prevalent on canals and turnpike roads would be followed, and they expected that private carriers would furnish vehicles and motive power and would pay a toll for the use of the line.

In practice, however, it was found impossible to work a railway on such principles. Steam-engines could not be allowed to use the track without regulation, and even with horse-drawn vehicles trouble frequently arose when the unregulated coaches met on a single track. Technically, economically, and historically, there are strong arguments in favour of the whole system being worked by one proprietor. In general this means undivided ownership, though some modifications to this rule still persist in regard to the ownership of the rolling stock or of leased lines.

## THE DEVELOPMENT OF RAILWAYS IN BRITAIN

The Stockton and Darlington Railway, opened on September 27, 1825, was the first public railway to be operated on modern principles. The transition from the old horse-drawn railway to the modern system of rail transport was very apparent on this line since the forms of motive power included steam-locomotives, horse traction, and cable traction. Until 1833 passengers were conveyed in horse-drawn coaches operated by independent proprietors. In the meantime the Canterbury and Whitstable Railway, opened May 3, 1830, gained the distinction of being the first railway to convey passengers in steam-hauled trains.[6]

Railways were not new in 1825. Many years earlier wagon-ways had been built in the colliery districts, and some of these, such as the Tanfield Colliery Wagon-way in County Durham, constructed in the early eighteenth century, were surprisingly like a modern railway, with cuttings and embankments provided to ensure a level track.[7] Iron rails and flanged wheels were used long before 1825, and experimental locomotives had been built by Trevithick, Blenkinsop, Hedley, Stephenson, and others. Even public

---

[6] See Rev. R. B. Fellows, *History of the Canterbury and Whitstable Railway*.

[7] Cf. W. W. Tomlinson, *The North-Eastern Railway*, and R. Davies, *The Railway Centenary*.

incorporation by special Act of Parliament was not new. The Peak Forest Railway had obtained such powers in 1794, and the Surrey Iron Railway was built in 1801 as a public railway which any one could use on paying the appropriate tolls. The importance of the Stockton and Darlington Railway lay not in the adoption of any one of these elements, but rather in their combination.

The second great landmark in the early history of railways was the opening of the Liverpool and Manchester Railway on September 15, 1830. The great success of this company proved the superiority of the railway over the canals and demonstrated the suitability of rail transport for the carriage of passengers. Though the first railways had been primarily inaugurated to carry coal, passenger traffic was found very profitable and yielded the bulk of railway revenues from 1830 to 1850. Numerous other lines soon followed, and by 1838 some 490 miles, including the first trunk line—the London and Birmingham Railway— had been opened in England and Wales. By that year also the G.W.R., the L. and S.W.R., and the Eastern Counties Railway were all under construction.

The railways, however, were not developed without strong opposition from canal companies and coach proprietors, which had to be appeased by lavish bribes or by the purchase of their stock at fancy prices. Even the turnpike road trusts had to be compensated for loss of revenue, e.g. in 1838 the Edinburgh and Glasgow Railway Company had to pay £25,000 to the various road trustees between the two cities. Landowners mulcted the railway companies of large sums for the compulsory acquisition of their lands or else the lines had to be diverted to avoid mansion houses or fox coverts. Towns such as Northampton objected to their amenities being disturbed by the building of railways or stations. Even preliminary surveys were carried out with difficulty, and Pendleton, in an account of the survey of the London and Birmingham Railway, tells us that ' the surveyors' most bitter and unrelenting foe was a clergyman. He would not at any cost permit a lot of rough men with strange instruments and mysterious antics, on his glebe. But the engineers were not easily daunted, and at last they cleverly out-witted him. The extraordinary expedient was resorted to of surveying his property during the time he was engaged in the pulpit—before he left the church the deed was done and the sinners had all decamped.'[8]

The press also was hostile; for instance, a writer in *John Bull* of November 15th, 1835, declared: ' We denounce the mania as destructive of the country in a thousand particulars—the whole face of the Kingdom is to be tat-tooed with these odious deformities; huge mounds are to intersect our beautiful valleys; the noise and stench of locomotive steam-engines are to disturb the quietude of the peasant, the farmer, and the gentleman; and the roar-ing of bullocks, the bleating of sheep, and the grunting of pigs to keep up one continual uproar through the night along the lines of these most dangerous and disfiguring abominations.'[9]

As a result of opposition and the extortion of vested interests, the capital outlay on British railways was greatly increased, and this accounts in part for the fact that British railways are the most highly capitalized in the world. But despite the opposition, the railways were rapidly extended, and by 1840 the main trunk lines had been built, and by 1850 a very extensive network of lines had been con-structed. By 1842 some 1,800 miles of railway were open; in 1845 some 2,400; in 1850 some 6,600; in 1858 some 9,500; in 1870 some 15,500; in 1890 some 20,000 miles.

Britain, however, suffered from the disadvantages of a pioneer and from the lack of any ordered policy of develop-ment. The railways were not built to any regular plan as in Belgium or France, but were constructed in a haphazard method to meet local requirements. Wasteful competition was encouraged by Parliament, and not until 1846 did the

---

[8] John Pendleton, *Our Railways*, Vol. I, p. 79.
[9] Quoted by E. A. Pratt, *History of Inland Transport*, pp. 246-7.

Government prescribe a uniform gauge for the various lines. The loading gauge of the early lines was small, and as compared with foreign railways, British railways still suffer from limitations on the width and height of their rolling stock and locomotives since it would now be too expensive to reconstruct tunnels, bridges, and other works.

But Britain gained immensely from her early construction of a railway network, and indeed it was an essential factor in her nineteenth-century industrial supremacy. Industrial expansion had been waiting on improved transport, and the railways enabled British manufacturers to work under conditions of large scale production and to locate their factories in the most favourable areas. Without the railways, coal mining could never have developed as it did, and in the nineteenth century cheap coal was the foundation of Britain's industrial supremacy. The iron, steel, heavy engineering, and shipbuilding industries were rapidly developed as a result of the provision of cheap transport. Before the railway age, Adam Smith, Napoleon, and others had described Britain as a ' Nation of Shopkeepers ', but now she had become ' the workshop of the world '.

### THE DEVELOPMENT OF FOREIGN RAILWAYS

In Belgium, railways were developed systematically as a national undertaking shortly after 1830. Belgium was well situated geographically to take advantage of the economic development of Europe, and she exploited her situation to the full by the construction of an elaborate railway network. ' In some ways Belgium led Europe in railway building. She was ahead of all the Continent in ordered construction, and ahead of England in that she had a railway policy when England was fumbling for a policy which she never found.'[10]

[10] J. H. Clapham, *Economic Development of France and Germany*, p. 140.

In Germany the great industrial expansion which took place after 1870 was due in large part to the extension of the European railway system. Previously Germany had made great strides in the development of her own internal railway system, a project which the eminent economist, Friedrich List, had strenuously advocated as early as 1833. Treitschke boasted, though perhaps with some exaggeration, that ' It was the railways which first dragged the nation from its economic stagnation : they ended what the Zollverein had only begun; with such power did they break in upon all the old habits of life that already in the 'forties the aspect of Germany was completely changed.'[11]

In America the railways greatly facilitated the development of manufacturing methods based on standardized production by automatic or semi-automatic machinery.[12] In the opening up of the West the railways played an important part, and this ' Westward Movement ' has been one of the most significant features of American economic development.

In America the railways were built for the most part to create new traffic, whereas in Europe they were constructed to provide in the first place for existing traffic.[13]

### BRITISH RAILWAYS AND THE TRADER

During the latter part of the nineteenth century the railways facilitated a new organization of retail trade, just as earlier they had revolutionized manufacturing methods. Traders were enabled to increase the variety of their goods since their capital could be laid out on small quantities of each article which when sold could be replaced at short notice by using rail facilities. The railways laid themselves out to provide for such retail trading, and they built up a quality of service unsurpassed by the railways of

---

[11] Quoted by J. H. Clapham, *ibid.*, p. 150.
[12] Cf. E. L. Bogart, *Economic History of the United States*, p. 452. (Second Edition.)
[13] Cf. E. R. A. Seligman, *Principles of Economics*, p. 575. (Eighth Edition.)

other countries. Small lots are accepted, rapid deliveries are arranged, cartage services are provided, and wagons are not held up, as in other countries, waiting for full loads. Such facilities naturally increase the operating costs of goods traffic, since they necessitate small wagons, low minimum consignments, and the handling of numerous small consignments. Foreign railways handle more bulk traffic, large consignments, and full wagon loads, though the tendency since the war has been largely in the direction of British practice.

| WAGON AND TRAIN LOADS IN TONS | | |
|---|---|---|
| | Av. wagon capacity | Av. load per wagon. | Av. train load (net). |
| Britain . . . . . | 11·3 | 5·64 | 130 |
| Germany . . . . . | 16·0 | 7·7 | 290 |
| United States . . . | 42·2 | 26·9 | 804 |

The success in Britain with which the railways have met the requirements of the home traders has been responsible for an increased demand for such facilities, as traders have learnt to expect and depend upon such services. During recent years the competition of road transport and changes in trading methods have greatly intensified the tendency.[14]

### THE FURTHER DEVELOPMENT OF RAILWAYS

In Great Britain there are some 20,400 route miles of railway open for traffic, equivalent in single track to 37,170 miles. In addition there are about 15,600 miles of siding, giving a total track mileage of some 52,770 miles. This gives approximately 46 route miles per 100,000 inhabitants, and 20 route miles of railway per 100 square miles.

It is doubtful if there is now any great scope left for

[14] See the author's *Transport Co-ordination*, Chapter I.

further construction apart from duplications of tracks, sidings, and extensions in new industrial regions. Indeed, as experience has proved during the past few years, many branch lines are really redundant owing to the competition of motor road transport. Development possibilities lie not so much in extension of route mileage as in improved organization, better operation, the adoption of new technical methods, and co-ordination with road transport. A review of present tendencies suggests many directions in which improvements will take place. Indeed, in the long period of railway depression since the war, the railway companies have made every effort to improve their technical equipment despite financial difficulties. Among recent improvements may be mentioned colour-light, automatic and power signalling; suburban electrification; hump shunting, automatic rail brakes and central control of points in marshalling yards; the introduction of co-ordinated road services; the mechanization of booking-offices as at Newcastle and Loughborough stations; and the application of mechanical appliances to statistical and accounting work.

Despite the progress which has been made by mechanical road transport since the war, it is an unquestioned fact that railway transport is still essential to our industries and commerce. It is not at all likely that the railways will be superseded. The railways, owing to the extent of their organization, can provide facilities which would be impossible with other forms of transport. The ramifications of the railways and the close co-operation which exists between the various companies enable services to be provided on a nation-wide scale, so that in effect every station, depôt, port, and private siding throughout the country is in communication with each other. By means of extended cartage areas and co-ordinated motor-bus services, these facilities can now be provided to almost every village, hamlet, factory, and farm-house in the Kingdom, while the successful operation of the Harwich-Zeebrugge train ferry has extended the effective range of rail transport even as far afield as France, Germany, Poland, Italy, and the Near East.

The railways are unrivalled for the carriage of heavy traffic, raw materials, bulky articles, or low grade commodities, and they can provide more effectively than other forms of transport for intensive passenger services, while for both goods and passengers the speed of rail transport gives it a great advantage on the long haul. The effective sphere of road transport, though considerable and still slowly expanding, is limited. That of inland waterways and the coasting trade is even more restricted, while traffic suited to air transport is but a very small fraction of total transport requirements.

| | Coal, Coke and patent fuel.* Tons. | Other minerals and goods traffic Tons. | Passengers. | | | Livestock. Number. |
|---|---|---|---|---|---|---|
| | | | Ordinary. Number. | Workmen. Number. | Season Tickets.† | |
| 1913 | 225,601,127 | 138,822,827 | 943,581,214 | 255,684,307 | 584,209 | 19,526,838 |
| 1923 | 222,234,412 | 121,032,196 | 925,265,018 | 310,301,402 | 893,668 | 17,266,293 |
| 1924 | 209,160,559 | 125,336,341 | 925,929,312 | 310,280,715 | 851,074 | 17,845,536 |
| 1925 | 193,661,991 | 122,289,259 | 923,996,458 | 308,584,456 | 851,229 | 18,662,650 |
| 1926 | 114,098,398 | 101,498,629 | 808,823,528 | 260,160,693 | 788,159 | 18,157,952 |
| 1927 | 195,769,382 | 126,079,933 | 887,758,974 | 286,980,183 | 793,791 | 19,727,620 |
| 1928 | 187,328,581 | 118,800,223 | 893,658,990 | 302,196,386 | 784,216 | 19,120,604 |
| 1929 | 207,130,109 | 122,448,634 | 926,765,117 | 309,447,415 | 780,902 | 17,700,802 |
| 1930 | 193,288,726 | 111,072,381 | 916,668,012 | 300,617,688 | 779,031 | 16,116,580 |

THE WORK OF THE RAILWAYS OF GREAT BRITAIN (ALL COMPANIES)

*Excludes free hauled.
†Equivalent number of annual season tickets.
*Note.*—Figures abstracted from Ministry of Transport, Annual Railway Returns.

In the above table the vast amount of work performed by the railways is shown, and to sum up we may say that industry and trade are still dependent on the railways for carriage of the bulk of their traffic, especially that in raw materials. In the carriage of passengers, the railways carry by far the greatest bulk, except on purely local journeys.

## CHAPTER II

# THE REGULATION OF RAILWAYS BY THE STATE

FROM the earliest days of railway enterprise, there has been in almost every country a very close contact between the railways and the State. Legislatures have been influenced in promoting control over the railways by a number of factors: (1) railways are in the nature of an important public utility; (2) railways, until the recent development of motor transport, had a virtual monopoly of the means of inland transport; (3) there was a danger that discrimination and undue preference might be practised to the detriment of certain industries, places, or individuals; (4) a railway must obtain powers to purchase land and easements under compulsion, as otherwise the construction might be held up by a single landlord; (5) in some countries political, administrative, strategical, or tariff policies have been important factors. Bismarck, for instance, declared unequivocally that 'it is impossible to carry out a customs tariff policy independently of a railway tariff policy'. These aspects have been strongly emphasized by German economists; for example, Professor Hermann Schumacher, in an article on 'The Nationalization of Railways in Prussia', said:

From the standpoint of the community at large the railways may be considered a 'means' in various ways. They may be thus considered from the general economic, the financial, the commercial-political, and the military point of view. They may be looked upon as a means of political power, of revenue, and of traffic. Of course, all these points of view have been taken into consideration in the nationalization of the Prussian railways, but the decisive and dominant factor was first and foremost the general economic aspect of railways as a means of traffic subservient to the development of the economic powers of a nation.[1]

In many countries the State itself has undertaken the construction and operation of railways; in others the State has exercised its regulative functions through the grant of concessions, while in those countries where Governments have been content to leave construction and operation in the hands of private companies, they have enforced strict regulations in the public interest. In no country has the State left the railroads to the unrestricted commercial exploitation of their enterprise. There are, of course, great differences in the form of this relationship, though, as Mr. Cleveland-Stevens has pointed out, there are, broadly, two main attitudes.

The attitude of Governments to railways may be described as positive or negative. The positive attitude is that of the chief continental States; it consists in aid to railway construction, definite assumption of responsibility for finance, of rights of interference, and of dictation as to management; in its logical sequence it extends to State ownership and working. The negative attitude is English; no assistance is afforded to companies; they are given charters which lay stress on what they may not do; interference takes the form of legislating against certain possible evils, not of planning general schemes for harmonious progress.[2]

THE PROMOTION OF A RAILWAY COMPANY IN GREAT BRITAIN

British railways are statutory joint-stock companies, and in certain respects they differ in legal status from ordinary joint-stock companies registered under the Companies Acts. Incorporation by Parliament was necessary in the early days of railway enterprise before the laws granting facilities for the formation of joint-stock companies were

[1] *The State in Relation to Railways.* Published by the Royal Economic Society (1912). See also E. A. Pratt, *Rise of Rail Power in War and Conquest* (1916).

[2] *English Railways: Their Development and their Relation to the State*, pp. 61-2.

passed. But even to-day an ordinary joint-stock company could not construct a railway, except perhaps for a very short distance, because special legal powers would be necessary to acquire land from unwilling landlords or to allow the line to cross public highways. In this respect railways are akin to other ' way-leave ' industries, such as tramways, telephones, telegraphs, gas, water, and electricity supply. Incidentally all these industries have certain other characteristics in common, since much fixed capital is required to provide a line of way, and monopoly operation is more economical than competition which would involve much duplication of capital.

Railways obtain their legal powers by means of special Acts of Parliament which confer certain privileges but also impose certain restrictions and obligations.[3] This procedure is very old and has been invoked by the promoters of water companies, canals, enclosures, and in connexion with the construction of river weirs, ports, highways, and turnpike roads. Applications for powers to construct and operate a railway take the form of ' Private Bills ', and if the application is granted these become ' Private Acts ', being so called to distinguish them from ' Public Acts of Parliament ' which affect the public at large or which concern the State itself.[4] Every British railway has been incorporated by a special Act, and the powers of the present grouped railways, except in so far as subsequent general railway legislation has modified the position, are derived from the original powers of a large number of small companies, each inaugurated by a special Act of its own.

[3] In Scotland, under the Private Legislation Procedure (Scotland) Act 1899, legal powers can be obtained by presenting a petition to the Secretary for Scotland asking for the issue of a Provisional Order, and, subject to certain conditions, an inquiry is held in Scotland before a Tribunal set up by the Act, instead of in Westminster. This procedure saves the expense of bringing officials and witnesses to Westminster, though if important matters are involved, Parliament may require the Provisional Order to proceed as a Bill.

[4] Private legislation is often subdivided into Local and Personal Acts according as it refers to definite localities, individuals, or groups of persons.

According to the Royal Commission on Railways of 1867, some 1,800 Acts of Parliament sanctioning the construction of new lines had been passed up to that time together with about 1,300 other special Acts modifying the provisions of the original Acts. As might be imagined, it was an extremely difficult task to ascertain the precise law affecting any company or any portion of its lines. Since then several general Acts, such as the Railway and Canal Traffic Act 1888 and the Railways Act 1921, have introduced greater uniformity, though sometimes it is still necessary to refer to the multitudinous early Acts regulating the constituent companies.

To obtain permission for the construction of a new railway or to extend or modify old powers, the promoters have to comply with the Rules or ' Standing Orders ' of both Houses of Parliament. These have been laid down by Parliament to facilitate parliamentary work and afford an opportunity for individuals whose interests might be adversely affected to bring their case before Parliament. The Standing Orders require that notices of any proposed Bill must be published twice in papers circulating in the localities affected and once in the London and Edinburgh Gazettes in the month of December previous to the session in which the Bill is to be introduced. Plans and sections of any proposed works, together with the names of all persons owning, occupying, or leasing the lands affected, must be recorded in a *Book of Reference* and deposited locally on or before November 20th. Notices have also to be served upon all owners, lessees, and occupiers on or before December 5th, informing them where they can see the plans and obtain copies of the Bill. The Bills themselves have to be deposited in Parliament on or before November 27th.[5] The Bill must also be read and approved at a meeting of the stockholders convened for this special purpose, which is known as a *Wharncliffe Meeting*, so

[5] The various dates have recently been advanced to those stated above in order to facilitate parliamentary work and to enable Bills to receive the Royal Assent before the Whitsun recess.

B

called after Lord Wharncliffe, who was responsible for this regulation.

Any person who has a *locus standi*, i.e. whose interests are affected, can petition Parliament against the Bill, and all such objections are considered during the committee stage. Where such opposition is designed to secure adequate protection to particular interests it is called ' *clause opposition* ', while objections against the Bill as a whole is known as ' *preamble opposition* ', since it is in the first sections of a Bill that the public case for the Bill is stated.  During the passage of the Bill through its various readings and committees, amendments may be introduced, obligations and restrictions may be imposed, or the Bill may be completely rejected.  Generally when a Bill is passed, certain general statutes are incorporated, such as the Railway Clauses Acts, the Companies' Clauses Acts, and the Land Clauses Act 1845.  These secure uniformity and obviate the necessity of repeating in each special Act a great number of provisions relating to land purchase and other matters.

In the Act as finally passed, it is usual to state first the special objects of the Act, then follow certain formal sections, one of which incorporates the General Acts.  The Act may next constitute a company and give it powers to construct ways and works, and to acquire land.  Detailed provisions are laid down to regulate the exercise of these powers and permission is given for the creation and issue of capital.  The Private Act thus brings the railway into existence as a company, giving it all the privileges of a corporate body, and determining its legal relations to the public, the stockholders, and the landowners.

A railway company is limited to the exercise of the powers contained in its special Acts, and it may not apply its funds to unauthorized objects nor engage in any business not permitted either explicitly or implicitly.  Enterprises may be undertaken which are on a reasonable interpretation ancillary or incidental to its main functions, but the company must not act *ultra vires*.

Procedure by Private Bills has been largely responsible for the growth of a haphazard system which was neither planned nor co-ordinated on any systematic basis, even the gauge of the various railways being unregulated till 1846.[6] Though the railways were granted powers for the compulsory purchase of land, they were not protected from the extortionately high prices demanded by landowners, and in this respect British railways have been much less favoured than those of other countries. Other important drawbacks of Private Bill legislation are the great expense involved, the amount of parliamentary time taken up, and the inelastic nature of the system.

### THE PROMOTION OF A LIGHT RAILWAY

By the Light Railways Act 1896 (as amended by the Light Railways Act 1912 and the Railways Act 1921) the Minister of Transport is empowered to make ' Orders ' containing all the powers necessary for the compulsory acquisition of land and for the construction of a light railway. These Orders have all the force of an Act of Parliament, but need not be referred to Parliament, since the Minister, at his discretion, may make or refuse an Order or refer it to Parliament. Financial assistance may be granted by the Central Government or Local Authorities. The procedure is that the promoters, after such notices and advertisements as are prescribed, lodge a *Draft Order* with the Minister, who, after hearing objections and holding an inquiry, may make an Order, incorporating any amendments which he considers necessary. The Order thereon acquires statutory force.

This special procedure was introduced to facilitate the construction of light railways in rural districts and reduce

---

[6] Stephenson's gauge of 4 feet 8½ inches was the most usual, but there was quite a diversity of gauge among early railways. Brunel of the G.W.R. had built to a 7-feet gauge; the Eastern Counties was originally 5 feet; the Kilmarnock and Troon 4 feet; the Edinburgh and Dalkeith 4 feet 6 inches; the Sirhowy 4 feet 4 inches and the Festiniog 1 foot 11½ inches.

the parliamentary costs involved. But no definition has ever been laid down as to what is a light railway, nor is it always possible to distinguish a light railway from a tramway or an ordinary railway. The Order may apply to a standard gauge railway as well as to a narrow gauge railway; it may limit the weight of the rails, the load permitted, or the speed of the trains, but there is nothing to prevent the construction of an ordinary railway under such an Order. In fixing the compulsory purchase price for land, the arbitrator may take into account any benefit which the landowner might obtain as a result of its construction.[7]

### THE LEGAL STATUS OF FOREIGN RAILWAYS

In continental countries, railways have long been classified according to their importance and standard of construction and equipment. Thus in Germany light railways in the technical sense of lines below the usual standards of construction and importance are called *Kleinbahnen*, in France *chemins de fer d'interêt local*, and in Belgium *chemins de fer vicinaux*.

In all these countries the State does not interfere with the management of the light railways, though it grants them financial assistance. In Germany the *Kleinbahnen* are worked by contractors; in France they are under the control of the Prefect of the department in which they are situated, and in Belgium the numerous vicinal lines are built and controlled by a national company in which the State, the provincial and communal authorities are shareholders, but they are worked by local contractors usually on leases for thirty years.

### RAILWAY REGULATION IN FRANCE

As regards standard railways in France, the State has largely contributed to the cost of construction by sub-

[7] See also Chapter IX, p. 111.

ventions, actual construction of works, or payment of interest on capital. Thus a large part of the fixed capital has been provided or interest on it guaranteed by the State, and the railways are more nearly on an equivalent footing to road transport than in this country.

The early lines were largely planned and constructed by the Government. They were then offered for competition among those willing to operate them, certain conditions being imposed and maximum charges prescribed. These concessions or leases were almost invariably for periods of ninety-nine years, after which the lines were to revert to the State. As competition for the concessions increased, new leases were reduced to thirty or forty years duration, but this tendency was reversed in 1852, when all the various concessions were extended to a uniform period of ninety-nine years from that date. In many cases the Government also guaranteed bonds issued by the companies, and moreover the railways were granted monopolies in their areas, constructions being limited to what was considered adequate to serve the needs of each district.

By a law of 1842 the State undertook the construction of earthworks, bridges, viaducts, tunnels, and stations. It also undertook responsibility for one-third of the cost of land, the remainder being found in instalments by the Departments and Communes through which the railways would pass. The companies therefore had only to provide the rails, locomotives, and rolling stock, and to maintain and operate this equipment. It was intended that in this way three-fifths of the total cost would be borne by the Central and Local Governments and only the remaining two-fifths by the companies. The various companies were amalgamated into six large groups, each with a practical monopoly in its area. At the same time a rigid system of State regulation and audit was introduced, and the obligation was continued which had required the railways to convey mails free of charge and to carry military and State employees at very low fares. Further strict and comprehensive regulations were laid down in laws of 1845 and 1846. So strict were these regulations that J. S. Jeans, writing in 1887, stated: 'There is indeed no country in the world where railway control has been more completely developed into a system of State interference than in France.'[8]

In 1922 the important Railways Act of that year retained the old six principal systems, five of which are company operated and one State operated, but attempted to standardize and co-ordinate their financial administration, wages, equipment, and operation. The State retained its controlling power over rates and policy, but set up a Supreme Railway Council consisting of sixty-one members, including representatives of the companies, the State railways, the employees, and the trading community. This Council is responsible for the general supervision of the railway systems of the country, including extensions, mergers, loans, tariffs, wages, and waterways. Machinery was also established to facilitate arbitration on wages questions and conditions of service. An executive committee was also set up, consisting of the President of the Council and two directors of each system.

### RAILWAY REGULATION IN GERMANY

The early German railways were constructed in some cases by companies and in others by the Governments. In Baden, Würtemburg, Bavaria, Hanover, Brunswick, and Hesse the railways, with few exceptions, were constructed and worked by the State Governments. In Prussia the Government encouraged private enterprise and granted various subventions, took shares or guaranteed interest on capital where private enterprise would not otherwise have been attracted. In 1838 the railways came under the control of the Council of Trade, and the companies were given powers to acquire land. The Government reserved the right to purchase any railway thirty years after its

[8] *Railway Problems*, p. 79. See also Lardner, *Railway Economy*, Chapter XVIII (1850).

construction at the rate of twenty-five times the annual dividends paid on an average of the previous five years. Rates and fares were controlled by the State, but the construction of competitive railways was not permitted. In 1871 new regulations applicable to the North German Confederation of States came into force, and in 1886 another set of regulations were introduced which established a most comprehensive code and dealt with every possible phase of railway construction and operation. In the decade 1880-1890 most of the railways, other than local light railways, were nationalized. After the Great War the whole of the German railways were nationalized in 1919 and consolidated into a single unit. In 1924, by the 'Agreement of London', the State Railway was handed over to a Commission to be operated so as to produce a surplus which would go to Reparation accounts, and is now known as the Deutsche Reichsbahn-Gesellschaft.

### STATE REGULATION IN THE UNITED STATES

In the U.S.A. railways obtain their legal powers from a charter granted to them by the State. Most of the charters are derived from the State Governments, though Federal incorporation is also permissible and has been granted to some of the Pacific railroads. Incorporation can be effected by a special Act of the State legislature, or in accordance with general laws. The latter have been passed by most of the States so as to prevent corruption and favouritism.

In the early days no general control was exercised by the Government and almost complete freedom of action was given to the railroads. Under the 'General Railroad Law' of New York State, for instance, any twenty-five or more persons could associate themselves for the purpose of providing a railway, and without any special application to the legislature, they became a body corporate empowered to construct, maintain, and operate a railway. This example was followed in many of the other States.

Such incorporation gave power to railways to take land for their lines on paying compensation equivalent to its market value. Those willing to build railways were thus encouraged because land in many parts was not long settled and the need for the construction of railways was felt to be urgent. But owing to the lack of control, abuses became frequent, and in time these led to a demand for strict regulation. In the West, during the ' Granger Movement ', the railroads were severely criticized on the grounds that the high rates prevented farmers from disposing of their products at remunerative prices. As a result of the numerous complaints, very severe laws were passed in certain States, but these were later repealed as they prevented further construction. Then Commissioners were appointed who were given varying powers to discover abuses and hear complaints, but until 1887 no adequate control was exercised by the Federal Government. In that year the Inter-State Commerce Commission was established to regulate the railways, and its powers were extended or more clearly defined by a series of Acts in 1889, 1893, 1903, 1906, and 1920. Its authority is now very extensive and it has imposed a very large measure of State control, extending to small details of traffic operation and commercial policy. In 1920 the Esch-Cummings Transportation Act laid down that rates and fares should be so fixed as to yield under economical and efficient management a fair rate of return (estimated at 5¾ per cent.) on a valuation of railroad property.

#### STATE REGULATION IN GREAT BRITAIN

British railway companies are regulated by their own special Act or Acts and by a long series of general Railway Acts. At first the State merely regulated the tolls which might be imposed because it was thought that the railway companies would only provide the permanent way and stations and that competition between private carriers would suffice to keep charges at a moderate level. Soon, however, the railway companies themselves undertook carriage, and gradually the independent carriers were eliminated. Still Parliament hesitated to interfere, since *laissez-faire* principles were then in the ascendant. *Laissez-faire* policy, however, assumed the presence of competition, but a monopolistic trend soon became evident in railway enterprise. The legislature therefore felt itself forced to interfere, and the railways were the first great modern industry to be regulated in detail by the State. At a later date the principle of regulation was imposed on other public utilities such as tramways, gas, and electricity supply, as these industries also showed a marked monopolistic trend.

Throughout the nineteenth century the problem of railway regulation bulked large, as the State, the traders, and the general public were apprehensive of the new monopoly and called upon the law to curtail and qualify its powers. Committee after committee and royal commission after royal commission were set up to investigate and report on the railway problem, and numberless Acts of Parliament were passed to secure regulation, culminating eventually in the Railway and Canal Traffic Act of 1888.

Gradually, as the century wore on, Parliament obtained a controlling power over the railways, and the possible dangers that might have arisen as the great companies obtained territorial monopolies were minimized, though at no time in our history have the grosser abuses of railway discrimination been permitted such as were at one time prevalent in the U.S.A., and though British railways have suffered from the heavy weight of official restrictions, they have also escaped the more onerous provisions enforced about 1900 by the Inter-State Commerce Commission of the U.S.A.

In the main, the various Acts regulating British railways may be grouped under the following heads: (1) Provisions as to rates, fares, and charges. (2) Provisions to secure reasonable facilities for the public. (3) Constructional and safety requirements. (4) Provisions forbidding undue preference and unfair or unreasonable contracts. (5) Provisions regarding amalgamations. (6) Provisions relating to accounts and statistics, and (7) Provision of facilities for the conveyance of Forces of the Crown, workmen, and certain other persons at cheap rates.

For convenience the main Acts relating to railways are briefly summarized below.

*The Railways (Conveyance of Mails) Act,* 1838. This Act required railway companies to provide adequate facilities for the carriage of mails.

*The Highway (Railway Crossings) Act,* 1839. This provided that railways must build and maintain gates at level crossings over roads and provide a person to open and shut the gates as required.

*The Railway Regulation Act,* 1840. Certain periodical returns were to be made by railway companies. Copies of all by-laws were to be laid before the Board of Trade and any of these might be disallowed by the Board. By-laws allowed under this Act include throwing bottles from moving trains, defacing of tickets, or travelling without a ticket.

*The Railway Regulation Act,* 1842. Notice was required before a railway was opened so that it might be inspected by Board of Trade officials who could order any improvements to be made if these were necessary for safe working.

*Regulation of Railways Act,* 1844. On every passenger line one train each way was to be provided every lawful day carrying passengers at 1d. per mile, stopping at all stations and travelling at a speed of not less than 12 m.p.h.

*Railway Clauses Consolidation Act,* 1845. Provisions of this Act have been generally included in special Railway Acts to avoid repetition of clauses which are usually inserted in Acts authorizing the construction of railways. The Act for example gave powers for alteration of water and gas pipes, construction of bridges over roads, temporary occupation of private roads and lands, etc. Another Act—the Railway Clauses (Scotland) Act, 1845—with similar provisions applies to Scotland. In the same year the Lands Clauses Consolidation Act and the Companies Clauses Act were also passed.

*The Railway Regulation (Gauge) Act,* 1846. This Act prescribed a standard gauge of 4 feet 8½ inches for all standard railways except in the west of England.

*Railway and Canal Traffic Act,* 1854. *(Cardwell's Act.)* Traffic to be received and forwarded without delay and without partiality. Any undue preference is forbidden.

*Regulation of Railways Act,* 1868. Uniform accounts were

to be kept by all railway companies. Tables of fares must be posted in stations. Smoking compartments to be provided on all passenger trains where more than one compartment of each class is provided (except on the Metropolitan Railway). Communication cords must be provided between the passengers and the guards. This Act also prohibited the running of special trains in connexion with prize fights.

*Regulation of Railways Act*, 1871. The Board of Trade was empowered to inquire into railway accidents, and returns relating to accidents were required. Inspectors were appointed for the purpose.

*Railway and Canal Traffic Act*, 1873. This Act set up the Railway and Canal Commission.

*Post Office Parcels Act*, 1882. Provides for carriage of parcels for the post office and the remuneration to which railway companies are entitled for such services.

*Cheap Trains Act*, 1883. Provided for a due proportion of accommodation on trains for passengers travelling at fares not exceeding 1d. per mile. Also for workmen's trains and conveyance of Forces of the Crown at reduced fares.

*Railway and Canal Traffic Act*, 1888. This provided for a scale of maximum rates and for a new classification.

*Regulation of Railways Act*, 1889. Block signalling and the provision of continuous brakes on passenger trains were made compulsory.

*Railway and Canal Traffic Act*, 1894. Railway companies were required to show that any rate or charge increased since 1892 was reasonable.

*Diseases of Animals Act*, 1894. Under this Act, the Board of Agriculture was empowered to make Orders regulating movement of animals when necessary to check or prevent disease.

*Light Railways Act*, 1896. A Light Railway Commission was established with powers to authorize construction of light railways.

*Railways (Private Sidings) Act*, 1904. Reasonable facilities must be afforded for the provision and working of private sidings.

*Railway (Accounts) Act*, 1911. Accounts have to be rendered in a prescribed and compulsory form along with certain statistics.

*Ministry of Transport Act*, 1919. This Act transferred the railway powers of the Board of Trade to the newly created Ministry of Transport.

*Railways Act*, 1921. This most comprehensive Act made revolutionary changes in many phases of railway regulation.

*Railway (Road Transport) Acts,* 1928. By these Acts, the four grouped railways obtained powers to operate road vehicles under certain conditions.

## MINISTRY OF TRANSPORT REGULATIONS

The requirements of the Ministry of Transport are very extensive, covering not only signalling, the length, width, and height of platforms, the rise and tread of steps, gradients at stations, the provision of continuous brakes on passenger trains, the erection of quarter mile posts along the lines, the running of mixed trains, and many other matters, but also descending to such minor points as the provision of clocks at stations, the showing of station names on lamps, and the provision of hand-rails on staircases and ramps. All passenger lines and stations before they are opened for traffic must be inspected and passed by the Ministry's Inspectors, as must any subsequent alteration of stations and signalling. The Inspectors have power to order any structural alterations or changes in signal equipment which they think necessary. The railway companies must notify the Minister of Transport of any accident which has caused, or might have caused, loss of life or personal injury to any person, and when the Minister thinks fit he can institute an inquiry and publish a report with observations and recommendations. Returns are also required regarding all breakages in service of important materials, such as rails, wheel tyres, axles, couplings, and draw-bars.

## ACCOUNTS AND STATISTICS

In the early days of railways, there were few regulations regarding the form of accounts, and the different companies adopted different systems. The Royal Commission on Railways of 1867 urged the desirability of a uniform system, and in the Regulation of Railways Act 1868 the form of the accounts was prescribed, but the different railway companies adopted different practices in allocating their expenditure and revenues to the various accounts. Following the report of a Board of Trade committee, both the form and basis upon which railway accounts should be compiled for publication were prescribed by the Railway Companies (Accounts and Returns) Act 1911. This has since been modified to some extent by the Ministry of Transport Act 1919, when ton-mile and passenger-mile figures were required for the first time, and by the Railways Act 1921. In December, 1928, certain minor modifications in the statutory form of the report were made by order of the Minister of Transport. The Royal Commission on Transport in their Final Report in 1931 recommended that the elaborate accounts and returns which the companies are required to make ' should be reviewed with the object of seeing whether the number of such returns might not be reduced and their form simplified '.

In the present statutory form of report which has to be presented by the Directors for each year ending 31st December, there are nineteen different accounts, with four further sub-divisions and sixteen statistical returns.

The financial accounts and statistical returns required in a railway report are as follows:

## PART I

### FINANCIAL ACCOUNTS

No. 1 (a) Nominal Capital Authorized and created by the company. The capital created is often less than that authorized since companies do not always seek subscriptions from the public to the full extent allowed.

No. 1 (b) Nominal Capital Authorized and created by the company jointly with some other company. This does not apply to all companies, e.g. L.N.E.R.

No. 1 (c) Nominal Capital Authorized and created by some other company on which the company either jointly or separately guarantees fixed dividends. The L.N.E.R., for instance, guarantees 67½ per cent. of the total fixed dividends of the Forth Bridge Railway Company.

No. 2. Share Capital and Stocks Created showing proportion issued. This account shows the amount of each type of stock issued, e.g. 4 per cent. First Guaranteed Stock, 4 per cent. Second Guaranteed Stock, 5 per cent. Preferred Ordinary Stock. The number and types of stock of course varies as between the different companies.

No. 3. Capital raised by Loans and Debentures.

No. 4. Receipts and Expenditure on Capital Account. This account shows on one side the total receipts on capital account from shares and stocks, loans, debentures, etc., and on the other side the amount expended on permanent way, rolling stock, workshops, road vehicles, steamboats, canals, docks, hotels, etc. Totals up to the previous year are shown, and to this is added the detailed figures for the current year.

No. 4A. Subscriptions to other undertakings, e.g. the L.N.E.R. has contributed £5,000 to the Derwent Valley Light Railway.

No. 5. Details of Capital Expenditure for the year ended 31st July. This specifies expenditure on new constructions, widenings, sidings, rolling stock, steamships, docks, etc.

No. 6. Estimate of Further Expenditure on Capital Account for the year ending 31st December following.

No. 7. Capital Powers and other Assets available to meet further Expenditure on Capital Account.

No. 8. Revenue Receipts and Expenditure of the whole undertaking. This shows the gross receipts, expenditure and net receipts for the ancillary enterprises as well as for the railway separately as required by the Railways Act 1921. It also shows the revenues derived from holdings in other companies.

No. 9. Proposed Appropriation of Net Revenue. This is naturally of much interest to the shareholders.

No. 9A. Statement of Interim Dividends paid.

No. 10. Receipts and Expenditure in respect of Railway Working. This is perhaps the most important statement from the point of view of railway economics. The table is very detailed and expenditure is allocated into its various parts and receipts are given separately for passenger, goods, mineral and other traffic. In a series of abstracts detailed figures are given for loco running expenses, traffic expenses, maintenance of stock and permanent way, etc. (lettered A to J).

No. 11 to No. 18. Receipts and Expenditure in respect of various ancillary enterprises, e.g. road transport, steamships, canals, docks, hotels, electric power and light, etc.

No. 19. General Balance Sheet.

## PART II

STATISTICAL RETURNS

In the second part of the Annual Report are grouped the various statistical returns required by statute. There are sixteen tables headed as follows:

1. Mileage of lines.
2. Rolling stock.
3. Horses and road vehicles.
4. Steamboats.
5. Canals.
6. Docks, etc.
7. Hotels.
8. Land, etc.
9. Other businesses.
10. Maintenance of way and works.
11. Rolling stock.
12. Engine mileage.
13. Passenger traffic and receipts.
14. Goods traffic and receipts.
15. Tonnage carried.
16. Summary.

In addition to the information required in the Annual Report, the railway companies have to render a large number of statistical returns each month showing the number of passengers carried, the tonnage and ton-miles of goods traffic, locomotive miles and hours, wagon miles, and receipts from particular commodities. At regular intervals, also, returns have to be furnished showing passenger-miles, cartage costs, marshalling-yard costs, and ton-miles for each length of haul for particular commodities.[9] About June of each year a bulky volume is published giving a comprehensive summary of the accounts and statistics for the previous calendar year.

[9] See Chapter IX, pp. 111-12.

### THE LAW OF UNDUE PREFERENCE

The Railway Clauses Act of 1845 laid down that tolls should be charged equally in respect of all traffic which was of a similar nature. This regulation was not of much practical importance, but in the Railway and Canal Traffic Act 1854 (Cardwell's Act) all undue preferences were definitely prohibited as follows:

> No company shall make or give any undue or unreasonable preference or advantage to or in favour of any particular person or company or any particular description of traffic, in any respect whatever.

By the Railway and Canal Traffic Act 1888 the burden of proof was placed on the railway company concerned to show that any charge was not an undue preference if it were proved that such a charge was lower to any trader or class of trader, or to the traders in any particular district, than to other traders for the same or similar merchandise or for the same or similar service. A like rule applies where any difference in treatment can be proved. Charges must not be higher for merchandise carried over shorter distances than for similar services over longer distances. The Railway and Canal Commission was given jurisdiction to enforce the law of undue preference, which function has been retained to it by the Railways Act 1921. The law of undue preference does not apply to traffic which the railway is not compelled to carry, e.g. railways are not common carriers for damageable goods, precious metals, wild beasts, or dangerous goods. Also it should be noted that preference in itself is not prohibited—it is indeed the very basis of the statutory railway classifications and of exceptional and special rates. What is forbidden is ' *undue* ' or ' *unreasonable* ' preference. Restrictions regarding preference do not apply to road transport undertakings, and thus railways are at a disadvantage with their road competitors in quoting rates. Exceptional rates by rail cannot be granted off-hand, since care must be taken to see that no undue preference is involved. Since 1854 there has been a great mass of litigation concerning undue preference, but now certain principles may be said to be fully established. Preferences may be justified on various grounds. Thus it might be shown that the expense of handling was reduced by better packing or because the traffic gave better loads. In other cases traders may offer large quantities of traffic or provide a regular supply of traffic. This would also apply to cartage services, and railways could charge more to traders who used such services only occasionally, though in practice the railway companies do not differentiate.

In certain cases it might be shown that the costs were greater because of gradients or similar reasons. Differences in costs of handling or working may be used to justify differences in rates between foreign and home goods, though if the services are similar, foreign goods must not be preferred to home. A complaint about alleged preferences to foreign goods in 1895 failed because it was proved that the commodities were delivered in large quantities from the ships and packed so as to take up little room in proportion to weight, while the trains could be run direct to London. Local produce, on the other hand, was delivered to the company in very small quantities, was badly packed, and had to be picked up at several stations.

Localities must not be unduly favoured, and in general, traders are entitled to the full benefit of their geographical situation or proximity to markets. It would therefore constitute an undue preference if the same percentage reduction were not given for exceptional rates to the same town from two different centres. On the other hand, low rates may be granted in order to bring a district into competition with another district provided that the difference in rates is not greater than is required by the necessities of competition.

Lower rates may be quoted between two places where there are competitive routes by rail, road, or sea, even though the route is longer or more expensive to work. Between intermediate stations, the rates need not be reduced

c

if traders are unable to take advantage of the alternative
route, and this difference does not constitute an undue
preference.[10]

In conclusion it may be said that generally a preference,
to be legally justified, must be based on a saving in cost,
or on a financial advantage to the railway concerned. But
such a preference must be available to all traders on the
same terms. In order to provide traders with information
of the rates available, the railways are bound to keep
a ' Rate Book' at every station and depôt open to public
inspection in which all rates to other stations are recorded.
The Rate Books give distances, scales of standard charges,
collection and delivery charges, and all exceptional rates
in operation from that station or depôt.

In regard to passenger traffic, undue preference is not
so important, as it is difficult to prove. All passengers,
however, in a like position must be treated the same.
Reduced fare tickets do not constitute an undue preference
provided they are available to all at the same terms, nor
is it held to be unreasonable to grant cheap season tickets
to traders who do a large business with the company.

#### UNDUE PREFERENCE IN THE UNITED STATES

At one time in the United States, undue preference was
rife, and even irregular or corrupt practices were not
unknown. Secret allowances were made to favoured
customers or to powerful monopolists; direct and indirect
rebates were freely granted; while another of the devices
was the ' midnight tariff ', whereby a special rate was
adopted for twenty-four hours only, expiring at midnight
on the first day of operation. The favoured trader would
be given previous notice, but the rate would be withdrawn
before other traders knew about it or could take advantage
of it. Such practices naturally raised a great outcry
against the railways, and in the subsequent agitation, even
quite legitimate discriminatory practices were condemned.

[10] See Chapter IX, pp. 108-9.

Eventually legislation stepped in to curb what had come to be felt as a gross abuse of monopolistic power. The Inter-State Commerce Commission Act 1887 prohibited undue preference, but this was not fully successful owing to subsequent legal interpretation of the ' long and short distance ' clause. Eventually the Hepburn Act of 1906, the Act of 1910, and other laws, provided for a strong and even drastic control over the railways.

## CHAPTER III

# THE INTERNAL ORGANIZATION OF A RAILWAY

RAILWAYS rank among the largest of commercial and industrial organizations, and their size prevents direct supervision of the widely separated parts of the organization and its scattered labour units. Moreover, many subsidiary and ancillary enterprises have to be provided, some of which, such as carting services, warehousing, or railway workshops, are indirectly involved in the movement of traffic by rail, while others, such as steamship services, docks, or golf courses, are provided with a view to obtaining traffic.

The L.M.S.R. employs some 232,000 persons; the L.N.E.R. some 180,000; the G.W.R. about 108,000; and the S.R. some 68,000, while the capitalization of each company ranges from £160,000,000 on the S.R. to £450,000,000 on the L.M.S.R. Such an immense labour force, and such a great capital necessitate an elaborate and comprehensive organization to provide for the supervision and direction of the work, the prevention of waste either in effort or materials, and the co-ordination of the various parts.

In the present century, great importance has come to be attached to problems of business organization and administration owing to the increase in size of business units and the greater complexity of modern production. Adequate organization facilitates production, increases the efficiency of labour and capital, eliminates waste, and is alert to seek out new methods and to adopt improved technical devices where these make for greater economic efficiency. Increasing attention is also being given nowadays to economic relationships between the executive and the staff on the one hand and between the firm and their customers on the other. These may be summed up under the words industrial conciliation and salesmanship.

Each industry has its own special technique of organization, varying in detail according to the nature of the business, and this specialized technique will be very different, for example, in the chemical industries, motorcar manufacture, publishing, or the railway industry. General principles of organization, of course, apply to all industries, such as division of labour or the law of substitution, but these need not be detailed since they are to be found fully described in any good text-book on economics.

### GENERAL FEATURES OF RAILWAY ORGANIZATION

Railway administrative problems naturally vary to some extent with the nature of the particular system. Compare, for example, the Canadian and the German railways. In Canada two great railway systems stretch for a distance of almost three thousand miles, on which most of the traffic is moving east and west along a narrow strip of country, while in Germany a single undertaking, constituting the biggest railway operating unit in the world, controls the entire railway system of a highly industrialized and thickly populated country.

The general features of railway organization in Britain are well known. The ultimate control, though this is largely nominal, rests with the stockholders, or, as they are called in accordance with long established precedent, the proprietors, except in so far as their powers are restricted by Parliament. The Directors, elected by, and responsible to the proprietors, are entrusted with the control of general policy, and from among their numbers a Chair-

man is elected to preside at the various meetings.   In
practice control is exercised by the Directors through
various Committees, since the amount of work involved
is very considerable.   The number and nature of the
Committees of Directors varies as between different
companies, but in general they are as follow:

(1) Traffic Committee responsible for supervising operating results.
(2) Finance Committee.
(3) Locomotive Committee.
(4) Works Committee dealing with permanent way,
   bridges, buildings, works, etc.
(5) Stores Committee.
(6) Land and Property Committee.
(7) Steamship Committee.
(8) Hotels Committee.

The decisions of the various Committees after they have
considered the matters before them in detail, finally go
before the full board.

The chief executive head is the General Manager (or
President as he is called in the United States and Canada),
who is appointed by the Directors.   His duty is to manage
the undertaking as a whole in conformity with the general
policy laid down by the Directors.   He is the pivot on
which turns the co-ordination of the various departments,
or divisions, and it is his task to hold the balance between
all the constituent parts of the organization in the general
interest of the railway company as a whole.   Under the
General Manager come the various officers who are charged
with the carrying out of the day-to-day work of the railway
organization.   The main problem of internal railway
organization is to obtain a satisfactory distribution of this
work.   There is first the question of ' Departmental ' or
' Divisional ' organization, which is perhaps the most
debated of all questions concerning railway organization.
The next important question is that of the precise line of
demarcation between the various duties.

### THE DEPARTMENTAL SYSTEM OF ORGANIZATION

In the early days of railway enterprise, the companies were sufficiently small to permit of the whole work of management being within the capacity of an individual, but as traffic grew and the size of the railways increased, some of the work of management had to be delegated. The question therefore arose: 'How was this to be effected?' Should one part of the work be separated and handed over to the control of an expert, or should the system be divided into areas under the supervision of an area manager who would be responsible for all the work in his area? The former solution is that of the departmental organization, the latter that of the divisional type.

In Great Britain the first alternative was adopted because in the early days it seemed clear that it was best to work the railway as a whole from a centralized headquarters. Moreover, the management of certain aspects or departments could be marked off definitely and placed under the charge of one individual, while the work of the specialists could be co-ordinated by the General Manager. The organization of all British railways developed more or less along these lines during the past century, and it must have suited British conditions, though it does not necessarily follow that it would be equally suitable in other countries, e.g. America, or under other conditions, e.g. much larger companies or in the face of road competition.

Neglecting minor differences, the following were the essential features of this organization. The General Manager was responsible to the Directors for the administration of the railway as a whole. Under him came the heads of four separate departments:

(1) The Civil Engineer (or Engineer) responsible for the permanent way, buildings, and signalling.
(2) The Mechanical Engineer in charge of the design, construction, and maintenance of locomotives and

rolling stock and supervising the carriage and engine-sheds.

(3) The Passenger Superintendent (or Superintendent of the Line) responsible for all passenger traffic working and the running of trains *both* passenger and freight.

(4) The Goods Manager in charge of freight traffic working, up to the time it left the goods station on the outward journey and after it had reached its destination station. In some companies there was also a special Mineral Traffic Department.

The railway system was divided up into a number of *districts* where representatives of the various departments, known as District Officers, were responsible for the work of their particular department and reported direct to their chief departmental officer. Sometimes the districts were called ' divisions ', but they were in no way equivalent to those which have given their name to the divisional type of railway organization.

The departmental system is a centralized form of organization, and the various officers are specialists in the work of their department. It is therefore claimed that they become more expert in their own particular work. At headquarters the chief officers can study their departmental problems as a whole and can prevent waste and overlapping as between different districts. But the system has also certain disadvantages. Much correspondence occurs between the various departments, and a good deal of time may be involved in referring questions to headquarters when several departments are involved. There is also a natural tendency among the various officers to regard problems from the point of view of their own particular department and not from that of railway working as a co-ordinated whole. Local officials who are most in touch with local affairs may be deprived of authority, and in this way public contacts may not be developed as they would where local officers had sufficient discretionary powers. Again, if friction developed between the departments, no decision may be reached till the problem comes for adjustment to the General Manager. This necessitates the General Manager being an all-round man having a technical knowledge of all departments.

The principle of specialization inherent in the departmental system is good, but against this has to be balanced a loss of elasticity and a less sure contact with local needs and conditions. Briefly it has the advantages of centralization, but there is a danger that it may become too centralized or top heavy and that too little responsibility may be given to the men in the districts. While the departmental system is very suitable for a small railway system, its limitations become more apparent as the railway becomes larger.

## MODERN BRITISH RAILWAY ORGANIZATION

Many changes have been effected in this earlier form of organization, especially since the amalgamations of 1921. Only the G.W.R., which has a compact area and which was least affected by the grouping, retains an organization which conforms roughly to this type. The main changes which have taken place are summarized by Mr. T. B. Hare as follows:[1]

(1) A re-division of work between the traffic departments.
(2) Re-division of work between the mechanical engineering and the traffic departments.
(3) Changes in the direction of giving greater responsibility to district officers.

## THE TRAFFIC DEPARTMENTS

Under the old system the actual working of freight traffic was effected by a department primarily concerned with passenger traffic. Responsibility for traffic movement cannot be divided, but as things were, serious delays might be

[1] *British Railway Operation*, p. 138.

caused to a goods train in order to give a slight advantage to an unimportant passenger train. There was also the possibility of insufficient co-operation between goods station staffs belonging to the Goods Manager's Department and marshalling yard staffs belonging to the Superintendent of the Line's Department. A division therefore was made between the actual carriage of the traffic and the various terminal services at either end. The former were brought under an *Operating Department* and the latter under a *Commercial Department*, which was subdivided usually into *Passenger* and *Goods Commercial*. The Operating Department deals with traffic movements over the railway lines. The Commercial Department is concerned with rates, fares, collection of charges, booking, advertising, refunds, invoicing, and cartage services. In the working of passenger traffic the line of division between the departments may be said to be drawn at the booking-office, and for goods traffic at the benches in the goods sheds.

This division has the advantage of being made on a logical basis, since one department is interested in revenue only and the other in working expenses only, but it has the disadvantage of separating into somewhat water-tight compartments what is really part of one complex whole. One department is in touch with the traders and passengers, but the other is not. One department may promise too much to traders without considering the cost involved to the operating department, while the latter, in the search for economies of operation, may stint facilities necessary to attract traffic. Mr. Lamb has suggested that districts should be reduced in size and District Traffic Managers appointed to combine both operating and commercial duties. Such officers would be responsible to both the Commercial Manager and the Chief Operating Superintendent. ' If there is any fault,' he states, ' with the English system it is in the separation in the districts of functions of securing the traffic and moving the traffic.'[2]

The commercial departments in the past have had gener-

[2] D. R. Lamb, *Modern Railway Operating*, p. 6.

ally greater power than the operating departments, and so a policy of obtaining traffic has overshadowed that of reducing running costs. No doubt an expansion of traffic reduces costs per unit, but sometimes the ' additional net cost ' occasioned by the extra traffic has been disproportionately great. Possibly the explanation is to be found in the keen competition for traffic and the high standard of service demanded by British traders. In France and Prussia, where the railways had a stronger monopoly, greater attention has been devoted to the reduction of operating costs, e.g. larger minimum wagon loads, shorter free periods of demurrage, slower transit times. In the U.S.A. a Vice-President of Transportation is usually appointed to co-ordinate and balance the revenue-producing and operating-expenditure sides of railway work. On British railways there is no such officer, unless it be the General Manager, though in the L.M.S.R. organization there is an approximation to this position.

THE ENGINEERING DEPARTMENTS

The Chief Mechanical Engineer has a position of considerable responsibility and importance since British railways manufacture most of their locomotives and rolling stock. In the past the C.M.E. was responsible for the design and construction of locomotives, their repair and maintenance, and the supervision of their running. It was claimed for this division of the work that engineers were best qualified to look after the locomotives and that experience of running under working conditions was useful to the designers. But the arrangement had the disadvantage that engine crews might regard themselves as independent of the traffic department, while the traffic department might not consider the effect of their demands on locomotive working costs or on the number of locomotives required. To secure more complete co-ordination, joint ' engine working committees ' were then set up. Later, many companies established a new department for Locomotive Running. The Locomotive

Running Superintendent was an independent officer in some companies, responsible only to the General Manager, but in others he was subordinate to the C.M.E. for constructional and maintenance duties and to the Operating Department in regard to train working. The advantage claimed for the special Locomotive Running Department was that an expert engineer could be put in charge, whereas the Operating Superintendent might have no special knowledge of locomotives. Mr. H. A. Watson has suggested that the formation of a special Locomotive Running Department merely increases the difficulties of the General Manager, and he advocates the handing over of locomotive running to the Operating Superintendent, except as regards sheds and shed duties. The shed foreman would be responsible to the Mechanical Engineering Department for repairs and maintenance, but to the Operating Superintendent for the running of locomotives and their preparation for duty.

On the L.N.E.R., responsibility is divided between the C.M.E. and a Locomotive Running Department, the latter having a chief officer in each area. The C.M.E. takes charge of design, experimental work, construction, and heavy repairs. On the L.M.S.R. the Chief General Superintendent—an operating official—controls the running sheds through assistants known as Superintendents of Motive Power.

ROAD-RAIL CO-ORDINATION COMMITTEES

A new feature in railway operating has been the formation of road-rail co-ordination committees since the Railway Road Powers were obtained in 1928. Joint committees consisting of an equal number of representatives of the railway companies and the motor-bus concerns associated with the railways have been set up in each area, and arbitration machinery has been established for use should the members fail to agree. The responsibilities of the various committees are the subject of special arrangements in each case, but in general they consider such matters as the closing of passenger stations and branch lines, the inter-availability of tickets, and facilities for combined road-rail travel.

### THE DIVISIONAL SYSTEM OF ORGANIZATION

In this type of organization the railway system is divided up into a number of divisions or areas, in each of which there is one responsible official in charge of all the work of the area—commercial, operating, and engineering.

The advantages claimed for the divisional type of organization are:

(1) Quickness in action and decision owing to the undivided local authority of the Divisional Manager or Superintendent.

(2) A saving in correspondence between departments and the elimination of duplicated effort.

(3) Reduction of friction as between departments and the possibility of substituting the team spirit for the departmental outlook.

(4) Responsibility can be allocated and blame for inefficiency cannot be passed backwards and forwards between different departments.

(5) Wider training of officials in the different branches of railway work.

On the other hand the same degree of efficiency cannot be obtained as there is less specialization. The employment of technical assistants may be necessary, and these may in effect become departmental officers communicating with each other through their chief. Staff matters are now negotiated in national agreements, and questions concerning rates and charges are discussed direct by headquarters with central traders' organizations. In Great Britain the departmental system has still probably the most advocates. They argue that though the mileage of the groups is very large, yet the areas which they serve are comparatively small, and therefore in conjunction with the extensive railway-owned system of private telephones, the departmental organization can work to advantage.

Against this there is to be set the possibility under a divisional system of a closer touch between local railway officers and the traders and public opinion in their areas. Mr. C. E. R. Sherrington therefore concludes that ' In these days of strong competition by road carriers, whose strength lies in their power to keep in touch with local opinion, such decentralization as is obtained by a divisional organization probably just tips the scales in favour of this form of organization.'[3]

Mr. T. B. Hare has suggested that the natural line of evolution for British railway organization towards the divisional type, if this is thought best, would be the combination of the whole of the traffic functions in one department and all the engineering functions in another.[4]

As regards the present position, the G.W.R. organization is very largely departmental, while the Southern Railway is also departmental, except that the operating department has charge of all operating functions other than the working of some of the larger goods stations, and the commercial department is concerned with both passengers and goods, including cartage. The L.N.E.R. combines the two systems, since the three areas under Divisional General Managers are of the divisional type, though within the areas the organization is departmental. The Divisional Managers who are responsible to a Chief General Manager have control of the way and works, hotels, steamships, property, and police, as well as the operating and commercial sides of the organization in their respective divisions. Locomotives, however, are under the control of the C.M.E., though their crews are controlled by Running Superintendents working under the Divisional General Manager in each area.

The L.M.S.R. has evolved an organization of its own which is partly divisional and partly departmental, and

[3] *Economics of Rail Transport in Great Britain*, Vol. II, p. 19.
[4] *British Railway Operation*, pp. 147-8.

in 1927 the organization was re-modelled somewhat on American methods. The President and the four Vice-Presidents form an executive committee responsible to the Board of Directors. The Vice-Presidents are in charge respectively of the operating, commercial, engineering, and financial departments. From time to time the President and Vice-Presidents meet as a committee to co-ordinate their work. The organization of work under the Vice-Presidents is departmental, but the whole control of train movements, including control of locomotives and their crews, is under one officer called the Chief General Superintendent. In 1931 the work of the Passenger and Goods Managers Departments was reorganized so as to give greater authority to local officers who were authorized to quote special rates and fares, to run special trains, to develop traffic, and co-operate with local associated road transport companies. An important feature of the reorganization was the improvement of telephone communications throughout the system. Later in the same year, the Executive Committee was reconstituted and the number of Vice-Presidents was reduced to three, responsible respectively for (1) the Railway Traffic, Operating and Commercial Section, (2) the Works and Ancillary Undertakings and (3) the Finance and Service Departments.

### AMERICAN RAILWAY ORGANIZATION

The divisional type of organization is usual in America, where indeed it originated. There the railways cover great areas, and one terminus may be thousands of miles away from the other, so that in consequence some sort of divisional organization is imperative. But in none of the systems is it completely divisional, just as in the British departmental system the station-master at least must be responsible for the work of several departments. In America, the Legal, Accountants', Secretary's, and certain other departments, are retained as such and centralized, but the traffic and operating work is decentralized on a divisional basis. The only large railroad which still retains a modified departmental organization is the New York Central Railroad. On other systems the Divisional Superintendents have control of all operating activities in their areas, including permanent way maintenance, engineering, and locomotive running. In some of the larger systems what is called a *regional organization* has been adopted whereby almost complete traffic and operating organizations have been established in each of several defined regions. The Pennsylvania Railroad, for instance, has established three regions, each under the control of a high official in the person of a Regional Vice-President.

## CHAPTER IV

# RAILWAY CAPITAL AND EXPENDITURE

## THE NATURE OF CAPITAL

THE term capital is a complex conception which would require many pages for a full analysis. Here only a brief elementary description of its nature and various forms can be attempted, and for a fuller description the reader should refer to some work on general economics.

British economists have generally distinguished between capital and land because in an old country, long settled, land, unlike capital, cannot be increased in quantity. But sometimes land is included under capital, and in considering the assets of a railway company, obviously the land owned by the company would be included as part of its capital. Capital is wealth saved and utilized to produce more wealth in the form of an annual income. Thus capital is contrasted with income, and capital costs can be likewise contrasted with annual expenditure. To start a railway, initial expenditure of wealth in the form of capital is required, and then each year, to keep it in working order, an annual expenditure is incurred. Capital could be compared to the trees in an orchard, while income can be compared to the fruit, and just as the trees have to be tended to keep them in good condition, and eventually have to be replaced when they grow too old, so capital has to be maintained and renewed from time to time.

Railway capital can be regarded in two lights, either as (1) the actual commodities used to provide the railway services, such as station buildings, locomotives, signals, permanent way, bridges, stores, etc., or as (2) the money value of these things.  The first view is that of capital in the concrete sense and is sometimes distinguished by calling these things ' *capital goods* '.  In the second the capital goods are valued in terms of money and this sum may be called the ' *capital value* ' of the railway.  In the one case we refer to the things themselves; in the other to their money value.  Money provides a common measure of values and is a convenient summary method for evaluating different things.  To enumerate the various items one by one would be a lengthy process and would involve complications, since allowance would have to be made for age, condition, size, and other variations.  The money measure, however, presents difficulties of its own when comparisons have to be made between different years during which the value of money may itself have changed.  The pound sterling is not now the same thing, for example, as it was in 1913 or in 1920.  Changes in the value of money also bring about changes in the relation of annual revenue to capital costs.  Before the war, for example, it took a railway about ten years to turn over its capital, but now it only takes between six and seven years.[1]  Again, though the same dividend may continue to be paid on capital over a number of years, it will represent different things if in the meantime the value of money has changed.

The nominal capital of a company may differ from the actual capital value of the various assets.  For instance, the nominal capital may be ' watered ', i.e. increased without a corresponding cash payment from the shareholders and without any addition to the company's assets.  It could not be said, however, that capital was ' watered ' if, for example, on amalgamation, the stock of an absorbed company was exchanged for a greater value of new stock yielding the same income, e.g. £100 stock which yielded 6 per cent. might fairly be exchanged for £150 of new

---

[1] In comparison a motor-bus concern can turn over its capital in about fourteen or fifteen months.

stock yielding 4 per cent. The average dividend on British railway stocks in 1929 was 4¼ per cent. and in 1930 about 3·7 per cent. of the value of the actual cash received from shareholders. On the other hand, the nominal capital may remain the same but the capital goods may be increased in quantity or quality by distributing each year less than the full net earnings in dividends.

Care must be taken to distinguish between capital expenditure and annual expenditure. The first represents the goods, or money, required to build and equip the railway, while the second represents the annual cost of maintaining and using the capital and includes such items as wages, salaries, cost of fuel, and depreciation.

Another important distinction is that between *Fixed Capital* and *Circulating Capital*. Fixed capital is that capital which is durable and can be employed many times in the service of the railway. Of course variations occur and some capital goods are practically indestructible, e.g. a cutting through hard rock; others last many years, e.g. a station, while yet others are comparatively short-lived, e.g. wheel tyres, rails, or brake couplings. Circulating capital, on the other hand, can only be employed once and is completely used up in the process of production, e.g. coal, oil, water, capital used to pay wages, etc. Much of the fixed capital of a railway has to be provided almost without reference to the amount of the traffic, and because of this fact it is often described as an *overhead charge*. The circulating capital, on the other hand, can be proportioned very much more closely to the amount of the traffic.

### THE NATURE OF RAILWAY CAPITAL

The outstanding characteristics of railway capital are:
(1) The large initial amount of capital necessary to provide the permanent way, stations, signalling, and other equipment. The total paid-up capital of British railways is about £1,200,000,000, while the value of the United States railroads has been estimated at about £4,470,000,000. In

comparison the capital required to inaugurate a road transport service is very low and may amount only to a few hundred pounds.

(2) Railway capital is not mobile, but once expended, is very largely tied to a particular route. If the railway proves unsuccessful, a great part of the capital is rendered worthless since it cannot be transferred elsewhere. In road transport operation, the vehicles represent the greatest part of the capital, and these are not tied down to particular routes like the railway. Road transport is a flexible form of transport, but a railway is more rigid.

(3) The proportion of overhead charges is very large, and these have to be incurred for the most part without reference to the amount of the traffic. Railways therefore thrive on a heavy, intensive traffic, but they are hard hit when working under capacity. Idle capital is the great bugbear of railway operating. The ideal to be achieved in all forms of railway operating is to use the capital equipment—permanent way, locomotives, carriages, wagons, stations, etc.—to the maximum extent possible.

#### THE CAPITAL OF BRITISH RAILWAYS

Owing to the high standard of construction, the expense of land, and the heavy legal and parliamentary costs, the capital outlay per route mile on British railways is very high. The average cost works out at about £52,040 per route mile, while in Belgium it is about £51,100, in Italy £41,720, and in Germany about £38,890. In the table opposite the amount of capital expended on British railways up to the year 1930 is shown.

In the table on p. 54 the distribution of the capital among the different items is shown, and in the last column the percentage which these bear to the total capital expenditure is indicated.

The capital goods which are represented by this capital expenditure include, among other things, 20,400 miles of route, equivalent to 37,170 miles of track, or, if sidings are included, 52,770 miles; 23,000 steam locomotives; 2,400 electric rail cars; 48,000 passenger vehicles; 690,000 merchandise and mineral vehicles, including brake vans; over 7,000 passenger stations; 35,700 road vehicles; 1,051 miles of canals; 81 hotels; 78 docks, and numerous steamships, totalling over 74,000 registered tons.

## BRITISH RAILWAY CAPITAL

|  | Total Capital Receipts. | Railway Capital expended. | Total Capital expended.* |
|---|---|---|---|
| L.M.S.R. . . | £429,776,826 | £384,152,206 | £452,281,721 |
| L.N.E.R. . . | £330,975,478 | £286,379,847 | £347,085,421 |
| G.W.R. . . | £167,258,455 | £145,482,083 | £175,630,028 |
| S.R. . . . | £156,027,926 | £139,101,289 | £159,389,717 |
| Total (4 groups) | £1,084,038,685 | £955,115,425 | £1,134,386,887 |
| Grand Total (all railways) | £1,187,479,062 | £1,068,593,533 | £1,234,037,483 |

* Includes capital spent on ancillary services and subscriptions to other companies.

NOTE.—The total capital expended exceeds the capital receipts from shareholders, etc., by about £46,500,000, since part of the profits earned in past years have been put back into the business.

### THE LAW OF DECREASING COST

It is seldom possible to keep the fixed capital of a railway fully employed, but in order to remunerate the large capital a considerable volume of traffic is necessary. The greater the traffic, the less is the weight of the capital charges on each unit of traffic. A railway is subject to the economic law of decreasing costs, or as it is sometimes called, the law of increasing returns. This law states that ' under certain conditions, an increase in production is effected at a decreasing cost per unit of output.' The law obviously applies where certain fixed overhead charges are involved. For example, in the publication of a book, the one type-setting would suffice whether 50 or 5,000 copies were printed, but

## DISTRIBUTION OF CAPITAL EXPENDITURE

| | L.M.S.R. | L.N.E.R. | G.W.R. | S.R. | Total. Four Groups | Percentage of Total Capital |
|---|---|---|---|---|---|---|
| | £ | £ | £ | £ | £ | |
| Permanent way and buildings | 311,845,886 | 232,996,318 | 120,687,541 | 119,220,624 | 784,750,369 | 69·2 |
| Rolling stock | 61,952,450 | 46,734,802 | 20,806,185 | 17,284,485 | 146,777,922 | 12·9 |
| Manufacturing & repair works | 9,955,443 | 5,949,867 | 3,952,857 | 2,437,937 | 22,296,104 | 2·0 |
| Lines under construction, leased lines, etc. | 398,427 | 698,860 | 35,500 | 158,243 | 1,291,030 | 0·1 |
| | | | | | | |
| Total Capital expended on railway | 384,152,206 | 286,379,847 | 145,482,083 | 139,101,289 | 955,115,425 | 84·2 |
| | | | | | | |
| Docks, harbours and wharves | 10,214,776 | 25,102,864 | 20,946,536 | 8,707,348 | 64,971,524 | 5·7 |
| Steamboats | 3,471,451 | 2,975,073 | 471,094 | 2,765,938 | 9,683,556 | 0·9 |
| Hotels | 5,172,709 | 2,640,115 | 181,334 | 1,627,559 | 9,621,717 | 0·8 |
| Canals | 5,949,632 | 1,313,118 | 781,668 | 77,700 | 8,122,118 | 0·7 |
| Road transport (vehicles, horses, garages, etc.) | 2,616,222 | 1,211,462 | 1,271,894 | 345,903 | 5,445,481 | 0·5 |
| Electric power stations | 2,024,835 | 449,651 | 516,696 | 685,863 | 3,677,045 | 0·3 |
| Lands, etc., not forming part of railway or stations | 15,292,080 | 12,240,382 | 3,139,640 | 5,668,305 | 36,340,407 | 3·2 |
| Lines jointly owned | 6,636,546 | 10,349,775 | 322,569 | 342,820 | 17,651,710 | 1·6 |
| Subscriptions to other companies | 10,321,508 | 3,238,711 | 2,451,980 | — | 16,012,199 | 1·4 |
| Miscellaneous | 6,429,756 | 1,184,423 | 64,534 | 66,992 | 7,745,705 | 0·7 |
| | | | | | | |
| Total Capital Expenditure | 452,281,721 | 347,085,421 | 175,630,028 | 159,389,717 | 1,134,386,887 | 100·0 |

in the latter case the proportion of the cost per copy would be very much less than in the former.[2] Likewise in the

[2] According to figures published by the Royal Economic Society in 1926, the cost of production of a certain book worked out at 8s. 6d. per copy for an edition of 500, at 5s. 3d. for 1,000, at 3s. 1d. for 3,000 and 2s. 4d. for 10,000.

case of the permanent way and buildings of a railway which account for about 70 per cent. of the total capital expenditure, the proportion of cost which must be set against each unit of traffic decreases as the traffic passing over the line is increased. This fixed capital invested in the permanent way, it is also to be noted, is provided for the traffic in general, and the cost cannot therefore be allocated against particular units of traffic.

Decreasing costs may also result from other economies of large scale production, such as in the case of the railway industry the use of larger wagons, increase in train loads, elimination of the wastes of competition, or economies in the use of circulating capital.

In railway operation the law of decreasing costs applies in a marked degree, though the applicability of the law is not always continuous. For example, as traffic increases up to the capacity of the line or that of the station and yard accommodation, the cost per unit of traffic decreases, but when the saturation point is reached, any further increase in traffic will necessitate the expenditure of more capital. No doubt for a time the expenditure of large sums of capital on track duplications can be staved off by various devices, such as an all-round increase of train speeds, the use of more powerful locomotives, or the erection of starting or advanced starting signals, etc. At this point, costs obviously are increasing per unit of traffic, and the economic law operating is that of increasing costs or diminishing returns. Eventually block sections will have to be increased, the lines doubled, or electrification adopted; all of which would involve great expense. But there would be no corresponding increase in traffic to set against the increased capital outlay and consequently costs per unit of traffic would go up with a jump on this section of line. But then as traffic slowly increases in following years, the law of decreasing costs would again make itself felt.

CAPITAL EXPENDITURE ON ROLLING STOCK

The capital invested by British railways in rolling stock amounts to about £155,000,000, representing about 13 per cent. of the total capital exclusive of some £36,000,000 representing private owners' wagons. This capital can be more readily proportioned to the traffic available than that sunk in providing the permanent way and other equipment of the route. Also it can be better allocated against particular traffic, e.g. passenger, mineral, goods, or live-stock.

Additional expenditure is involved in the case of goods traffic by the need of providing special wagons for particular kinds of traffic, e.g. elephant vans, insulated meat vans, banana vans, timber wagons, cattle trucks, or gunpowder vans. The aim has been to attract traffic from competitors, to provide for new types of traffic, or to reduce operating costs. The development of the electrical industry, for example, has necessitated the building of 70-ton transformer wagons. To meet the increasing demand for the transport of exceptionally heavy articles, the L.N.E.R. recently put into service a well-trolley wagon built to carry 110 tons, or in special circumstances 150 tons. In order to obtain the maximum use of special wagons and to reduce the numbers required to the minimum, the various railway companies have instituted systems of direct control over the movements and distribution of these wagons.

Where traffic is seasonal, difficulties arise in providing vehicles to meet peak requirements. These difficulties are especially acute in countries where one main crop is harvested in a period of a few weeks, e.g. wheat in Canada or maize in South Africa. In Britain the problem of seasonal traffic is especially difficult on the passenger side during Bank holidays, trades holidays, or wakes weeks. On Bank holidays the problem is acute, but during local holiday periods some relief can be obtained by transferring stock from one district to another. The big groups are better placed in this respect than their predecessors of pre-war days, when a line like the Highland Railway was sometimes forced to hire stock from other companies. The capital invested in goods and mineral wagons could be decreased if it were feasible to adopt larger capacity wagons,[3] and it is of interest to note that the average capacity of wagons has risen steadily from 10·35 tons in 1922 to 11·3 tons in 1930.

## ANNUAL EXPENDITURE

Annual expenditure is the money disbursed out of earnings to meet the recurrent charges for working and maintaining the railway. Annual expenditure has risen greatly since 1913 owing to the increase of wages, the adoption of the eight-hours day, and the rise in the price of materials. In 1913 the annual expenditure incurred by all the railways amounted to £75,456,530, whereas in 1930 it was £170,830,536 (all railways), or £162,602,689 for the four grouped railways. These figures include ancillary services, but taking railway expenditure only, the figures in 1930 were £147,595,684 (all railways) and £139,482,437 for the four groups. In the table on p. 58 the distribution of railway expenditure and the percentage on each item is shown for the year 1930.

In the table on p. 59, which has been taken from the *Railway Newsletter* of July, 1931, a comparison is given of expenditure in 1913 and in 1930. The second column for each of the two years shows in what proportions each pound of gross revenue was spent on the different items. In 1913 salaries and wages accounted for 36·25 per cent. of the total revenue, but in 1930 they absorbed 55·42 per cent.

In order to facilitate economic analysis, Sir William Acworth suggested that the various items of railway expenditure might be reclassified into a more logical order as follows:

[3] See Chapter XIII, pp. 170-3.

(1) General charges.
(2) Maintenance of way and works.
(3) Maintenance of rolling stock.
(4) Expenses of conducting transportation, i.e. locomotive running expenses and traffic expenses.

ANNUAL EXPENDITURE ON BRITISH RAILWAYS, 1930
FOUR GROUPED COMPANIES ONLY
(*Excludes expenditure on ancillary services*)

|  | Expenditure, | Per cent. of Total. |
|---|---|---|
| Maintenance of ways and works | £19,824,314 | 14·2 |
| Maintenance of rolling stock    . | 24,978,489 | 17·9 |
| Locomotive running expenses    . | 33,594,208 | 24·1 |
| Traffic expenses    .    .    . | 48,541,024 | 34·7 |
| General charges    .    .    . | 5,016,481 | 3·6 |
| Legal and parliamentary expenses | 201,668 | 0·1 |
| Rates, taxes, etc. .    .    . | 1,412,911 | 1·0 |
| Railway Freight Rate Rebate Fund* | 4,096,660 | 2·9 |
| Compensation    .    .    . | 897,813 | 0·6 |
| National insurance .    .    . | 1,243,239 | 0·9 |
| Total expenditure in respect of railway working    .    . | £139,482,437 | 100·0 |

* Under the Local Government Act 1929 the railways were 'derated', but had to pass on the saving by way of rebates in the charges for coal, coke, and patent fuel traffics (rebate 1½d. per ton and 27½ per cent. of remainder of the carriage charges); agricultural traffics (rebate 12½ per cent. of carriage charges); and iron, steel, and other selected industrial traffics (rebate 15 per cent. of carriage charges).

The general charges amounted in 1930 for the four groups to £5,016,481 as shown previously, or to 3·6 per cent. of the total expenditure. They include the fees and expenses of directors (£105,876 or 0·07 per cent. of total expenses), salaries of headquarters staff (£1,464,538), headquarters office expenses (£270,465), and like expenditure. All of these have only a slight and indirect connexion with the amount of traffic carried and the revenue earned by the railway.[4]

The cost of maintaining the ' ways and works ' amounted to £19,824,314 or 14·2 per cent of the total expenditure, and this increases as traffic increases, but at a much slower rate. Sir William Acworth calculated that about three-fifths of the cost of maintaining the permanent way is

| EXPENDITURE AND GROSS RECEIPTS, 1930 (FOUR GROUPED RAILWAYS) | | | | |
|---|---|---|---|---|
| Items of expenditure | 1913 | | 1930 | |
| | £ | Proportion per £ | £ | Proportion per £ |
| Salaries and wages | 46,956,000 | 7s. 3d. | 109,202,000 | 11s. 1d. |
| Materials | 26,593,000 | 4s. 2d. | 37,364,000 | 3s. 10d. |
| Rates, taxes, and Nat. Insurance | 5,322,000 | 10d. | 7,571,000 | 9d. |
| Sundry items (*less* miscellaneous receipts) | 5,035,000 | 9d. | 4,655,000 | 6d. |
| Available for interest and dividends | 45,219,000 | 7s. 0d. | 37,716,000 | 3s. 10d. |
| Total gross receipts | £129,125,000 | 20s. 0d. | £196,508,000 | 20s. 0d. |

independent of the traffic passing over the line, since it is largely worn out not only by traffic, but also by the weather. Increased traffic, therefore, does not cause a proportionate increase in the cost of maintaining the permanent way, and this illustrates one application of the law of decreasing cost to railways. Though the average

[4] Cf. Acworth, *Elements of Railway Economics*, Chapter IV.

percentage of expenditure on permanent way and works is 14·2 per cent. of gross expenditure, this is composed of somewhat varied figures for the various groups. The L.M.S.R. spent 12·82 per cent. of its income on its way and works in 1930, the L.N.E.R. 13·24 per cent., the G.W.R. 15·48 per cent., and the S.R. 19·1 per cent. Presumably the higher percentage in the case of the S.R. is due to the extent of electrified lines which have to be maintained.

Maintenance of rolling stock amounted to £24,978,489 or 17·9 per cent. of total costs in 1930 and includes the renewal and repair of locomotives, coaching vehicles, and wagons. This expenditure obviously is closely connected with the amount of traffic carried, though obsolescence may also be a cause of expense under this heading.

The last item, the expenses of conducting transportation, is not easily allocated between different kinds of traffic because many of the items are incurred in respect of the traffic as a whole. Even a broad division between passenger and goods traffic cannot always be made, as a large part of the expenses is common to both, e.g. signalling.

### GROSS AND NET RECEIPTS

Gross receipts consist of the total annual income obtained by a railway company from all kinds of traffic and from the various ancillary enterprises. Net receipts are the total gross receipts less all working expenses. The proportion of receipts absorbed by working expenses in any period is known as the ' *operating ratio* '. In 1914 this worked out at about 65 per cent., but since the war it has risen considerably beyond this owing to increases in wages and the price of materials. In 1923 the operating ratio was 83·25 per cent., in 1926 it was 90·36 per cent., in 1927 80·83 per cent., in 1929 it fell to 79·53 per cent. owing to the 2½ per cent. reduction in wages and salaries, but when this reduction was restored it rose to 81·78 per cent. in 1930. The operating ratio gives an index of the

## GROSS RECEIPTS IN RESPECT OF RAILWAY TRAFFIC. YEAR 1930.

| | L.M.S.R. £ | L.M.S.R. Per cent. of Total | L.N.E.R. £ | L.N.E.R. Per cent. of Total | G.W.R. £ | G.W.R. Per cent. of Total | S.R. £ | S.R. Per cent. of Total |
|---|---|---|---|---|---|---|---|---|
| Passenger Traffic | 20,370,294 | 30·14 | 13,484,184 | 25·96 | 9,019,834 | 30·75 | 14,125,483 | 63·80 |
| Mails, parcels, etc., by Passenger Train | 6,846,900 | 10·13 | 4,884,160 | 9·40 | 3,330,181 | 11·36 | 2,438,141 | 11·01 |
| Merchandise (Classes 7 to 21) | 20,124,197 | 29·78 | 14,311,407 | 27·55 | 7,985,446 | 27·22 | 3,053,992 | 13·80 |
| Minerals and Merchandise (Classes 1 to 6) | 6,087,838 | 9·01 | 5,254,004 | 10·11 | 2,439,491 | 8·32 | 854,967 | 3·86 |
| Coal, Coke, and Patent Fuel | 13,362,625 | 19·77 | 13,455,485 | 25·90 | 6,199,690 | 21·14 | 1,583,029 | 7·15 |
| Live Stock | 794,106 | 1·17 | 503,186 | 1·08 | 354,881 | 1·21 | 83,696 | 0·38 |
| Total Traffic Receipts | 67,585,960 | 100·00 | 51,952,426 | 100·00 | 29,329,523 | 100·00 | 22,139,308 | 100·00 |
| Total Passenger Train Receipts | 27,217,194 | 40·27 | 18,368,344 | 35·36 | 12,350,015 | 42·11 | 16,563,624 | 74·81 |
| Total Goods Train Receipts | 40,368,766 | 59·73 | 33,584,082 | 64·64 | 16,979,508 | 57·89 | 5,575,684 | 25·19 |

## GROSS AND NET RECEIPTS. WHOLE UNDERTAKING, INCLUDING ANCILLARY ENTERPRISES. YEAR 1930.

| | Gross £ | Net £ | Operating Ratio |
|---|---|---|---|
| L.M.S.R. | 76,445,101 | 11,976,709 | 84·33% |
| L.N.E.R. | 59,825,409 | 10,619,309 | 82·25% |
| G.W.R. | 34,346,867 | 6,120,390 | 82·18% |
| S.R. | 25,890,141 | 5,188,421 | 79·96% |

efficiency of a railway company's operations, but it is only a rough guide, since wages or prices may change, thus causing variations as illustrated by the fluctuation noted above. Also it is not necessarily a guide to dividend-earning capacity, because the volume of traffic may be too small to enable a dividend to be paid. The net income which remains after meeting working expenses, interest on loans, or debentures and other prior charges is available for paying dividends to the stock-holders, though part of this may be reinvested in the undertaking or placed to reserve.

### RAILWAY DIVIDENDS

The debenture holders have a prior claim on the net income, and if their interest is not paid they have a right to appoint a receiver to take over the management of the company.

Railway companies' capital is split up into a number of *shares*, usually of £1 in value, though when such shares are in large blocks they are generally known as *stocks*. The market value of the shares depends on the demand and supply and does not necessarily remain at their par value. In practice fluctuations in the value of the shares are generally governed by the prospect of dividends, as indicated by the weekly variations in the published traffic receipts. Recently, for example, deferred ordinary shares in a British railway company were selling as low as £3 or £4 for £100 of stock.

For many years railway stocks were greatly favoured by small investors and they have also been recognized by law as trustee securities.[5] Their popularity was due to the steady dividends, the wide market available ensuring

[5] The number of railway shareholders in 1929 was approximately 784,000, of whom 480,000 held stock of only £500 or under. Some shareholders may have held stock in various companies, but on the other hand many large investments, e.g. by insurance companies or friendly societies, represent a large number of investors.

ready sale at short notice, and the fact that they were easily split up into small amounts. Recently, however, the financial depression and loss of traffic has caused a falling off in the demand for railway shares. Some companies, indeed, have only just managed to retain their prior stocks, i.e. preferred and guaranteed stock, as trustee securities, since this requires that dividends shall have been paid on ordinary stock each year for ten years.

Railway shares are of different types according to the order of priority in payment of dividend. First come the Guaranteed Stocks with a fixed dividend of about 4 per cent. Then Preference Stocks with about the same return. Thirdly there are ordinary shares which rank after the others but are not restricted to a fixed percentage if profits are sufficient to enable more to be paid. The higher average yield of some ordinary shares before the war thus represented a payment for the extra risks involved.

The L.N.E.R. has split its stock up into as many as seven different classes (excluding debentures), but the other companies have been content with five or six classes of stock. This division of stock into different categories has been adopted with a view of attracting various types of investors. The order of priority of the various types of L.N.E.R. stock is as follows:

(1) 4 per cent. First Guaranteed Stock.
(2) 4 per cent. Second Guaranteed Stock.
(3) 4 per cent. First Preference
(4) 5 per cent. Preference (redeemable in 1955).
(5) 4 per cent. Second Preference.
(6) 5 per cent. Preferred Ordinary.
(7) Deferred Ordinary.

The ordinary stocks of the L.M.S.R. and the G.W.R. were not split into preferred and deferred ordinary stock because it was thought that the larger market for consolidated stock would make them more saleable.

As regards the rate of dividends, this has generally been

low even in the days of railway prosperity as compared with the returns in other industries, but before the war the returns were steadier and less liable to fluctuation than those of more speculative investments. The railways have been able to raise their capital cheaply with consequent benefit to the general public and traders.

### DIVIDENDS ON ORDINARY STOCK

|  | 1924 | 1927 | 1928 | 1929 | 1930 |
|---|---|---|---|---|---|
| L.M.S.R. ... ... ... ... | 7% | 4¾% | 3½% | 4½% | 2% |
| L.N.E.R. Preferred Ordinary | 5% | ⅜% | ¼% | 3% | ¼% |
| L.N.E.R. Deferred Ordinary | 2½% | nil | nil | nil | nil |
| G.W.R. ... ... ... ... | 7½% | 7% | 5% | 7½% | 5½% |
| S.R. Preferred ... ... ... | 5% | 5% | 5% | 5% | 5% |
| S.R. Deferred ... ... ... | 3½% | 2% | 2% | 2½% | 1¼% |

## CHAPTER V

## RAILWAY LABOUR

THE railway industry ranks as one of the most important employments of labour in Great Britain. In 1930 the railway companies employed directly some 632,000 persons, whose wages or salaries aggregated about £109,000,000 for the year. This labour force is extremely diversified and represents almost every conceivable occupation and employment.

### RAILWAY WAGES

Wages may be regarded subjectively or objectively. On the subjective side, regard is had to the utilities which the labourer obtains in return for the disutility of his toil. Any extra disutility tends to be rewarded by extra wages, as has been described by Adam Smith in his celebrated enumeration of the natural causes of differences in wages.

The five following are the principal circumstances which, so far as I have been able to observe, make up for a small pecuniary gain in some employments and counterbalance a great one in others. First, the agreeableness or disagreeableness of the employments themselves; secondly, the easiness and cheapness, or the difficulty and expense of learning them; thirdly, the constancy or inconstancy of employment in them; fourthly, the small or great trust which must be reposed in those who exercise them; and, fifthly, the probability or improbability of success in them.[1]

All these differences may be illustrated from the wide range of railway employments. Thus night duty, being

[1] *Wealth of Nations,* Book I, Chapter X.

more disagreeable than day labour, is generally paid at higher rates; the trained engineer gets more than the plate-layer, while the responsible duties of guards, signalmen, and drivers so far tend to increase their rate of wages over similar employments involving less responsibility.

To the worker, the main consideration is the *real wage*, i.e. the amount of commodities or services which he can obtain in spending his wages. In this connexion the purchasing power of money is important, and the object of introducing a cost-of-living bonus (known as the ' A ' scale) in 1920 was to stabilize the real wages of railway workers. In addition, when comparing the real wages of a railway-man with those of men engaged in other industries, account should also be taken of any special advantages of railway employment, or extra items of income such as free passes, privileged tickets, tips, uniform, superannuation, company's houses at reduced rentals, cheap coal, or paid holidays. Another important advantage of railway employment is the permanent character of the work available to most of the employees. Mr. Rowe calculates that before the war railway workers could count on overtime earnings of 5 to 10 per cent. in excess of weekly wages, whereas in other industries the worker might have to allow about the same net amount as a deduction from wages through unemploy-ment and short time.[2] It is true that some casual labour is employed, e.g. in goods sheds, but this is limited as compared with most other industries. Workshop staffs do not enjoy full security of tenure, but employment is some-what more regular than in outside industries.

Money wages were low in some departments before the war, but the popularity of the railway services was shown by the fact that often the same family took employment with the railways from generation to generation. During and after the war, however, railwaymen's wages rose con-siderably, and weekly earnings (including overtime and other payments) were increased still more. Mr. Rowe gives the following figures as representing the ' true '

[2] J. W. F. Rowe, *Wages in Theory and Practice.*

weekly wage rates (i.e. including small items of income, uniform, bonuses, etc.) for certain grades of railwaymen.[3]

|  | WEEKLY WAGE RATES | | | |
|---|---|---|---|---|
|  | 1886 | 1913 | 1920 | 1926 |
|  | s. d. | s. d. | s. d. | s. d. |
| Engine-drivers | 39 7 | 42 11 | 103 0 | 88 1 |
| Goods Guards | 27 6 | 30 9 | 84 6 | 66 5 |
| Goods Porters | 20 0 | 22 1 | 72 11 | 49 1 |

From the objective point of view, wages are regarded as a payment for so much work performed. The employer is mainly concerned with the cost of the work, and more highly paid labour, if proportionately more efficient, would be really cheaper than less efficient, lower paid labour. The cost of supervision of labour is also important, and with ' cheap ' labour this may be increased. Important problems are involved in the maintenance of discipline. Generally one or two methods have been used to check irregularities, viz. (a) suspension from duty, fines, etc., and (b) the record system whereby merit or demerit marks are accumulated, and if the latter exceed a certain number the man concerned is dismissed.[4]

### METHODS OF PAYING WAGES

The amount of work done may be measured in various ways, and in practice there are a great variety of methods of paying wages. Broadly, these may be divided into four groups: (1) *Time Wages*, paid by the hour, day, or week without direct reference to the amount of work done; (2) *Piece Wages*, i.e. payment by result, where the wage is directly related to the output of the worker; (3) *Task Wages*, where the time is fixed in which a set piece of

[3] *Wages in Theory and Practice*, p. 41.
[4] On the whole question see K. J. Norman Browne, *Brown and Other Systems of Railway Discipline*.

work must be performed; and (4) *Bonus Wages*, in which a premium, or bonus, additional to the fixed time wage, is paid according to the output.

On the railways, time wages are by far the most usual method of remuneration, since in the operating and traffic departments the workers are engaged in providing services which cannot be measured or assessed as could the output of specific commodities. Except in the workshops, it is seldom possible to adopt piece wage systems, though some examples are to be found, e.g. mileage rates paid to certain enginemen. Generally also there is a wholesome tradition among skilled railway workers that the job is there to be done, and the workers take a pride in their craftsmanship.

Owing to the difficulty of adopting piece wage systems, bonus schemes have been advocated for certain tasks where such an incentive stimulates efficiency. In goods sheds, a bonus is sometimes paid for each unit of work performed above a definite speed. The main difficulty is to find a suitable unit for measuring the work done. ' Consignments handled ' would not be suitable since packages differ so much in size and weight. If ' wagons loaded ' were selected as the unit, insufficient loading or careless stowing might result. This last disadvantage is also present when ' hundredweights dealt with per man-hour ' are taken as the basis, though on the whole this provides the best measure of the actual work performed.

Generally the bonus does not commence until a certain minimum tonnage is handled, but this minimum must not be set too high, as otherwise the incentive may be lost. The minimum might well be based on the normal amount of traffic handled during the week by the gang, and for every additional ton loaded or unloaded a bonus of say 9d. per ton might be distributed among the members of the gang.

Bonus systems are advocated because they afford a stimulus to work and encourage co-operation between the loaders, checkers, and porters comprising the gangs, but against this has to be set the cost of more careful supervision. In special circumstances, a bonus system may justify itself even if there is no direct saving in cost to the company. Thus quicker loading might obviate the necessity for expensive extension of goods sheds.

In some sheds, the bonus system is extended to the cartage staffs on the basis of tonnage handled. There are possibilities also for the introduction of bonus systems in connexion with the operation of motor vans and lorries, so as to encourage economies in petrol consumption and care of tyres.[5] This illustrates the application of the bonus principle as a stimulus to saving in materials or care of equipment, whereas in the first example the aim was to increase output.[6]

Bonus schemes have also been introduced to some extent in connexion with carriage cleaning, cattle wagon cleaning, loading of coal, marshalling yard working, and the operation of 'pick-up goods trains'. In the last case, the bonus is paid to train men on a graduated money scale corresponding to reductions in total journey time. Some of the trains have been completely re-timed, the men's previous earnings being guaranteed and the bonus paid if the trains are worked to their booked time or less.[7]

## THE RAILWAY TRADE UNIONS

Until the end of the nineteenth century, railwaymen played hardly any part in the general trade union movement.[8] This was probably due to the difficulty of organizing workers of varying degrees of skill and of different occupations, scattered in small numbers all over the country. But once organized, the railway trade unions

[5] See the author's *Economics of Road Transport*, Chapter VI, pp. 79-80.
[6] Before the war, bonuses were sometimes paid for good time-keeping, freedom from accident, etc.
[7] In one scheme of this nature a bonus of 3d. each is paid to the driver, fireman and guard for every quarter-hour by which they reduce their over-all time. The company hope to gain from a reduction in engine hours.
[8] S. and B. Webb, *History of Trade Unionism*, p. 523.

became very powerful, and the strike weapon in their hands, until the development of motor transport,[9] was of especial strength since almost the entire economic life of the community could be held up. In some countries, e.g. Canada, the legislature has therefore forbidden strikes among railwaymen or other workers in public utility services until the question in dispute has come before a Conciliation Board.

The first railway trade unions were formed in 1865 and 1866 among guards and locomotivemen on the N.E.R., while in the former year Charles Basset Vincent, a railway clearing house clerk, also organized a union. But all these unions were short lived. In 1872 Michael Bass, M.P., a large railway shareholder, helped to form the *Amalgamated Society of Railway Servants*, generally referred to in abbreviated form as the A.S.R.S. This was an *industrial union* rather than a *craft union*, since in theory at any rate it included railway workers of all grades and occupations. Though in its early years it had a chequered existence and was rent by internal dissensions, it was the first railway union to attain any degree of permanency. In 1880 the *Associated Society of Locomotive Engineers and Firemen* (the A.S.L.E. and F.) came into being, by the amalgamation of several small societies which had sprung up during the two previous years. About the same time, the *Scottish Society of Railway Servants* and the *United Pointsmen and Signalmen's Society* were established. The former was not very successful, and in 1892 it combined with the A.S.R.S.

In the 'eighties trade unionism was spreading among unskilled workers and the *General Railway Workers' Union* was formed to organize all grades, paying particular attention to the unskilled. Trade unionism did not spread among the clerical workers until a much later date, but in 1897 the *Railway Clerks' Association* (the R.C.A.) was established with a membership of 297.

Until comparatively recently, the railway trade unions

[9] On this subject see G. Glasgow, *General Strikes and Road Transport.*

were mainly concerned with reduction of hours of work, compensation for accidents, protection against ' victimization ', and with the friendly society activities. Statutory recognition of their claims to be protected against excessive hours was obtained under the provisions of the Railway Regulation Act 1893, whereby the Board of Trade was empowered to inquire into complaints relating to excessive hours of work, insufficient rest periods, or insufficient Sunday relief. In 1900 the Board was given further powers to make rules relating to the safety of workers.

The next stage was definitely inaugurated in 1907 when the A.S.R.S. presented an ' *All Grades Programme* ' for increased wages and improved conditions of service. As a strike seemed imminent, a conference was convened between representatives of the Government, the railway unions, and the railway directors, and an agreement was signed on November 6, 1907, which established a ' Scheme for Conciliation and Arbitration on questions relating to rates of wages and hours of labour of certain classes of railway employees '.

In 1911 a strike led to the appointment of a Government Committee to investigate the working of the conciliation scheme, and as a result of its report the conciliation boards were modified so as to secure more expeditious consideration of any question referred to them.

In 1913 the *National Union of Railwaymen* (the N.U.R.) was formed as an ' all-grades ' union by the amalgamation of the A.S.R.S., the Pointsmen and Signalmen, and the General Railway Workers' Union.[10] It commenced with 267,000 members, but by dint of a very thorough organization this membership was increased to 481,000 in 1919. The Locomotivemen's and the Railway Clerks' Association decided to retain their separate identity, but they have

[10] An attempt was also made by means of the ' Triple Alliance ' to link up with the Miners' Federation and the Transport Workers' Federation. These three unions are closely related and a stoppage of work in any one involves the other two in distress. Relations did not prove harmonious and in 1921 the Alliance broke up. Cf. Cunnison, *Labour Organization*, pp. 72-3.

co-operated with the N.U.R. in matters affecting their mutual interests. The N.U.R. opens its membership to all grades, including locomotivemen, clerks, railway road transport workers, and workshop employees, but these extensions of its activities have led at times to friction with other unions. Such conflicts illustrate the difficulties of organizing an industrial union which cuts across the more usual trade union organization based on occupations. The argument of the N.U.R. is that such work is incidental to, and in some respects inseparable from, the business of railway transport and that the railways, with all their auxiliary enterprises, must be regarded as an indivisible whole if anomalous differences are to be avoided.[11]

Just before the outbreak of war the unions were preparing to present a new ' all grades programme ', but on the outbreak of hostilities a ' *Truce Agreement* ' was reached under which existing conditions were stabilized. During the war, bonuses were granted at various dates to meet the increased cost of living, and in December, 1918, the Government granted an eight-hours day to all members of the wages staff and set up a committee to review rates of pay and conditions of service.

#### THE AGREEMENT OF 1919

In April and June, 1919, agreements were effected between the ' Railway Executive Committee ', acting on behalf of the Government, and the N.U.R. and the A.S.L.E. and F. providing for improved conditions of service for employees in the Conciliation Grades (i.e. practically all the wages staff except those in the workshops).

This agreement provided for:

(1) *A Guaranteed Day* whereby a full day's wage was guaranteed for each day a man was available for rostered

[11] See *Decisions of the Industrial Court*, Vol. IV, Part III, 1923. Decision 728, pp. 70-113.

duty or, in the case of trainmen, for each time of signing on duty.

(2) *A Guaranteed Week* consisting of forty-eight hours whereby a standard week's work was guaranteed to all men available throughout the week, exclusive of overtime, Sunday, or night duty.

(3) Overtime at the rate of time-and-a-quarter for work in excess of eight hours, each day standing by itself.

(4) Between 10 p.m. and 4 a.m. the rate of pay was increased to time-and-a-quarter, and any overtime between these hours was payable at time-and-a-half.

(5) Sunday work at time-and-a-half except for certain duties performed by permanent-way men, which was to be at double rates.

(6) Six working days with pay to be allowed as holidays each year.

(7) Twelve hours' rest to be allowed between turns at home stations and nine hours when away from home.

In August of the same year the wages of drivers, firemen, and cleaners were standardized on a service basis. Enginemen remaining on a mileage basis were granted a day's wage for 120 miles running, and thereafter, for each additional 15 miles, were to be remunerated at the rate of one hour's pay. Subsequently in 1923 the basic mileage was raised to 140 miles for a day's pay. After the strike of 1919 a settlement was reached on October 5th whereby wages were to be stabilized without change until September 30, 1920. In March, 1920, further negotiations resulted in the fixing for each conciliation grade of a standard, or ' B ' rate, 100 per cent. above average pre-war rates together with a current or ' A ' rate, representing the standard rate plus the existing war bonus of 33s. per week. The ' A ' rate was subject to variations according to changes in the Ministry of Labour Cost of Living Index Number on the basis of 1s. change in wages for each variation of 5 points in the index number. In no case, however, were wages to fall below the standard or ' B ' rate.

Somewhat similar agreements were also reached regarding standard rates of pay and conditions of service for clerks, station-masters, controllers, and supervisors.

It has been computed that additions to the cost of labour since 1913, including the extra staff necessitated by the adoption of the rigid eight-hour day, involved an addition of about 150 per cent. to the pre-war wages bill. In 1927 this amounted to £125,000,000 as compared with £50,000,000 in 1913, and this after allowing for charges in the price level representing an increase of about 50 per cent. on pre-war costs.[12]

### THE RAILWAYS ACT 1921 AND CONCILIATION COUNCILS

Part IV of the Railways Act 1921 provided for the establishment of conciliation boards somewhat on the lines of the ' Whitley Councils ' set up in certain other industries. As a result of the development of the railway trade unions and the adoption of this conciliation scheme the railways have now the most highly developed form of collective bargaining yet established in any industry.

The railway conciliation machinery consists of a National Wages Board, a Central Wages Board, Sectional Railway Councils, and Local Departmental Committees. The decisions of the various councils are not legally binding on either party. This is an important feature which fosters a spirit of goodwill and has the further merit of keeping the State out of industrial disputes. The scheme has worked very well up to the present and, with one exception, the decisions have been loyally accepted by both parties even when awards have not satisfied their claims.

*The National Wages Board* is composed of six representatives of the railway companies and six of their employees, two from each union, together with four representatives of railway users; one each from the Parliamentary Committee of the Trades Union Congress, the Co-operative Union, the Association of British Chambers of Commerce, and the

[12] W. V. Wood, *Railways*, pp. 158-9.

Federation of British Industries. This Board forms the apex of the conciliation hierarchy and is distinguished from the other boards by having members drawn from outside the railway industry itself.

*The Central Wages Board* is composed of eight representatives of the railway companies and eight of the railway employees, four elected by the N.U.R., two by the A.S.L.E. and F., and two by the R.C.A. Under Section 62 of the Railways Act 1921 the Board may consider questions relating to rates of pay, hours of duty, and other conditions of service referred to it in default of agreement between the unions and the companies. In the event of failure to agree, the questions may be referred to the National Wages Board.

Below the National Wages Board and the Central Wages Board a comprehensive system of railway councils has been set up as follows:

*Local Departmental Committees,* consisting of not more than four representatives of each side, were established in April, 1922, at stations and depôts in which the number of regular employees exceeded 75. These committees provide a recognized means of communication between employees and local railway officials and serve to give employees a wider interest in the conditions under which their work is performed. They consider such matters as the arrangement of working hours, holidays, safety appliances, and the loading of traffic. Where they fail to agree, the matter may be referred to the Sectional Railway Council concerned.

*Sectional Councils* represent various groups of grades and consist of not more than twelve members from each side. Their functions include the local application of national agreements relating to standard salaries, wages, or conditions of service as well as matters remitted by a Railway Council. It was also intended that they should consider suggestions relating to operating efficiency, staff welfare, the securing of traffic, and other matters of mutual interest.

*The Railway Councils* were established under Section 63

of the Railways Act 1921, one for each railway company and consisting of not more than ten representatives from each side. They deal with questions of common interest to more than one Sectional Council and with matters remitted from any Sectional Committee.

### RECENT DECISIONS OF THE NATIONAL WAGES BOARD

In 1931 the railway companies approached the National Wages Board for a reduction in wages, the abolition of the guaranteed day and week, reduction in overtime rates, and the adoption of a spread-over system in place of a straight shift of eight hours. Counter proposals were made by the Unions regarding the pay of certain grades and improvement in conditions of service.

In March, 1931, the National Wages Board recorded its findings, and these were accepted by both parties as the best obtainable in the circumstances. The main changes which were then introduced modified the 1919 agreement as follows:

*Conciliation wage grades.* (1) *Overtime.* A rate of time-and-an-eighth was substituted for day overtime in place of time-and-a-quarter. For night work the old rate was reduced to time-and-a-quarter. (2) *Night Duty.* A rate of time-and-an-eighth was substituted for time-and-a-half. (3) *Sunday Pay.* Time-and-a-third in place of time-and-a-half. Where double time used to be paid, the rate was reduced to time-and-two-thirds. (4) *Hours of work.* A ' spread-over ' up to twelve hours per day was permitted for all grades except drivers, firemen, guards, and signalmen subject to review in respect of any station where it was contended that such a spread-over was unreasonable. (5) Earnings were subject to a 2½ per cent. reduction with a further 2½ per cent. in respect of all earnings in excess of 40s. per week. In the case of male adults where basic rates were under 41s. per week, it was provided that deductions should not operate so as to reduce earnings below their basic rate and in no case was the deduction to exceed the sum of 6s. per week.

*Clerical, Supervisory, and Other Salaried Staff.* All earnings of these classes were subject to a deduction of 2½ per cent. with a further deduction of 2½ per cent. in respect of all earnings above £100 per annum, provided that in no case should any deduction exceed the sum of £15 per annum. Staff in receipt of salaries exceeding £350 per annum do not come under the Wages Board, but it was intended to introduce corresponding modifications in these salaries.

The guaranteed day and week were retained and some slight increases were granted to certain grades, e.g. crossing-keepers where it could be shown that their work had increased owing to the growth of motor transport.

The decisions were to operate from March 28, 1931, to March 26, 1932, and thereafter until altered by agreement between the parties themselves or by decision of the National Wages Board.

#### THE TRAINING AND SELECTION OF STAFF

The training of staff is now a recognized feature of big business, and considerable developments have taken place on the railways in this connexion. The London Underground Railways, for instance, have established very efficient training schools for this purpose. Many railway tasks can naturally only be learnt by long experience, but a course of training at the beginning of a man's career will enable him to profit more quickly from his experience and will save him from learning bad methods of work which later he may have to unlearn. Moreover much railway working is highly complicated and a knowledge of underlying theory and principles is essential. For many years, therefore, the railway companies have provided courses of instruction in locomotive driving and maintenance, the vacuum brake, block signalling, station accounts, and other subjects. Facilities for more advanced study among members of the clerical staff who desire to prepare themselves for administrative and managerial responsibilities in later life have also been arranged in connexion with many of the English and Scottish Universities and courses are now available in railway law, railway economics, railway operating, and railway geography. The earliest university classes in railway subjects were those started by the London School of Economics in 1895, and in this work the late Sir William Acworth was a pioneer. The Institute of Transport, founded in 1919, by means of its local sections and examination schemes, has done a great deal to promote the scientific study of transport problems among the younger men. In addition, the valuable work which is performed by associations such as the Railway Debating Societies and the Railway Students' Associations in London and Edinburgh deserves to be mentioned. The L.N.E.R., under its Traffic Apprentice Scheme, gives special training covering a period of three or four years to selected members of their staff and university graduates.

The extension of training schemes to members of the staff who come in contact with the public appears to present considerable possibilities, and it has been found most successful in certain other industries, e.g. tramways and large stores. A courteous staff can do much to improve public relationships and even to attract traffic to the railway. It is true that individual railwaymen often act up to the very highest standards, but specific training in courtesy would raise the general average.

During the past few years the German State Railway Company has carried out interesting experiments in the application of psychology to the selection of their staffs. It is claimed for the new methods that they eliminate those who are unfitted for the various kinds of work and enable the company to place entrants in the work for which they are best suited. Similar psycho-technical methods for occupational selection have been adopted by the Austrian Federal Railways.

### WELFARE ORGANIZATIONS

Nowadays increasing attention is being paid by large businesses to the welfare of their staffs both during and out of working hours. The railway companies have been among the first to recognize the importance of this work, which promotes the health, comfort, and general well-being of the staff as well as their efficiency. Among the facilities provided may be mentioned the canteens and dining-clubs established at large stations and works; the various housing schemes and the Railway Savings Banks which offer attractive facilities for saving. On the social and recreational side there are sports grounds, libraries, club-rooms, institutes, and horticultural societies. Each company publishes attractive staff magazines containing information of special interest to railwaymen. ' Suggestion Schemes ' have also been established with very successful results and monetary rewards are made to those whose suggestions are adopted. Encouragement is also given to the growing of flowers, shrubs, etc., at stations, and prizes are awarded for the best kept stations. Finally a special tribute must be paid to the voluntary work of the numerous ambulance and first-aid classes.

## CHAPTER VI

# RAILWAY AMALGAMATION AND COMBINATION

THE economic advantages of amalgamation are of especial importance in the railway industry because competition involves a wasteful and unnecessary duplication of a great amount of fixed capital. It is not surprising therefore that an economic urge towards combination is evident throughout the history of British railways from the time of the Wigan amalgamation in 1834 up to the Railways Act 1921. Over a thousand railways have been promoted in this country, but as a result of successive amalgamations there are now only four big groups and about ninety other lines. The wastes and expenses of competition between railways were soon discovered, and indeed it was foreseen by George Stephenson from the first; ' Where combination is possible,' he said, ' competition is impossible.' The elimination or reduction of competition has been effected in a variety of ways, and Mr. W. A. Robertson, in a study of this movement, enumerated ten distinct methods of combination.[1]

## FORMS OF AMALGAMATION AND COMBINATION

The various forms of combination and amalgamation may be summarized as follows:

(1) Complete amalgamation involving the purchase of a smaller concern or the complete merger of two or more companies into a single whole, e.g. grouping under the Railways Act 1921.

[1] *Combination among Railway Companies*, pp. 27-54.

(2) Promotion of joint lines, owned by two or more companies and managed by a joint committee, e.g. the Cheshire Lines Railway formed in 1865.

(3) Working unions authorized by Parliament which are managed and operated as a single unit, though each company retains its identity and capital. There is a common fund for all revenue and expenses, but net receipts are divided in fixed proportions according to the agreement. In 1899, for example, a working union was formed by the South-Eastern and the London, Chatham, and Dover Companies.

(4) Leasing of a line to another company which operates and keeps it in repair. This form of combination was common until parliamentary restrictions were imposed, e.g. the Eastern Counties Railway leased the Norfolk Railway in 1848.

(5) Working agreements for the operation and management of a railway by another company. This is very similar to a lease.

(6) Running powers whereby a company obtains the right to run its engines, carriages, and wagons over the lines of another company.

(7) Pooling agreements have been very numerous and are one of the most important forms of combination In 1850, for example, the eight companies then interested in traffic between England and Scotland introduced an extensive pooling arrangement. In its simplest form, receipts from traffic between two or more competitive points are divided in agreed proportions, but in more complicated forms of agreement, the principle is applied to all competitive traffic arising on the systems and not merely that between two or three definite points.

(8) Agreements not to promote competing railways have also been formed. Such an agreement seems to have been arranged in 1891 between the Caledonian Railway and the North British Railway.

(9) Through the Clearing House Conferences, various companies were able to come to agreements regarding

F

rates and fares on competitive routes. In this way the companies ceased to bid against each other for the custom of traders, though competition in facilities remained keen. The Conferences also controlled the grant of exceptional rates, since if any such rate is competitive in its nature it has to be referred to the appropriate conference.

(10) Joint Claims Committees were set up about 1902 to prevent undue leniency in the treatment of claims for loss or damage. Competition in rates having been eliminated, there was a tendency to attract traders to particular lines by less strict interpretation of the regulations and claims were often granted after little investigation. But after 1900 the companies found that the cost of such claims was excessive, but they could only take effective action by mutual agreement.

### AMALGAMATIONS BETWEEN 1844 AND 1847

The year 1844 may be taken to mark the beginning of the movement towards railway combination in Britain. Before that date there had only been three amalgamations: the first in 1834, a second in 1835, and another in 1840. By the amalgamation of 1834 the North Union Railway was formed by the fusion of the Wigan Branch Railway with the then uncompleted Preston and Wigan line. But none of the three first amalgamations was of any great importance as they involved the extinction of only three small companies, owning, all told, but thirty-three miles of line.

Consolidation and amalgamation were first initiated on an effective scale during the years 1844 to 1847 by George Hudson, ' the Railway King '.[2] He realized that combination was essential for financial success and efficiency of operation, while he also saw that facilities for through traffic were urgently required. Hudson had a powerful

[2] It may be of interest to note that Hudson was responsible for the installation of what was probably the earliest tuba stop on an organ. The idea was derived from a set of musical pipes fitted to one of his locomotives.

personality, but his financial methods were somewhat open to suspicion and eventually he was driven from power and influence. Nevertheless he did much to promote the greater efficiency of British railways by evolving extensive systems out of a chaos of small, competing companies. His outstanding promotions were the amalgamations which created the Midland Railway in 1844 and the L.N.W.R. in 1846. Both of these rank among the most important mergers in the whole history of British railways. In 1844, in addition to the Midland fusion, there were two other amalgamations, effected respectively by the G.W.R. and the North Union. In 1845 another three amalgamations were sanctioned by Parliament, one being the absorption of the historic Liverpool and Manchester Railway by the Grand Junction.

In 1846 the high water mark of amalgamations in this period was reached. Eighteen Acts were passed by Parliament to facilitate amalgamations, including the formation of the L.N.W.R. by Hudson out of a union of the London and Birmingham, the Grand Junction, and the Manchester and Birmingham. The Manchester and Leeds Railway (renamed Lancashire and Yorkshire Railway a year later) absorbed five other companies; the Midland Railway increased its importance by absorbing three more lines, while the L.B.S.C.R. was formed by a fusion of the London and Brighton and the London and Croydon.

The year 1846 was indeed an outstanding year in the history of British railways, since in addition to the numerous amalgamations, many lines were leased, numerous canals absorbed, and a record number of Railway Bills for new lines were promoted in Parliament. In that year also Parliament appointed a committee to consider the problem of railway amalgamation and attempted to set up a permanent body to control the growing power of the railways. There had been a lull in railway promotions after the financial crises of 1837, but after 1843 there was a great revival of railway constructions and the annual number of projects increased rapidly till 1847. The years 1845-7 were the period of the ' Railway Mania ', during which railways were planned in all parts of the country, many of which had later to be abandoned. There was a wild speculation in railway shares during the mania until the boom suddenly collapsed in 1847. But before this crisis put an end to further constructions, all the main lines of communication had been constructed.

## SUBSEQUENT AMALGAMATIONS

After 1847 amalgamations practically ceased to be effected for some years, though a considerable number were mooted. The most important exception was the formation in 1854 of the N.E.R. by the fusion of three companies. Parliament had come to regard amalgamations with strong disfavour, and was more eager to promote competition than to restrict it by increasing the monopolistic strength of the companies. Numerous committees were set up to investigate the question of amalgamations and various boards were established to curb the power of railway monopoly, but in actual fact the effective control of Parliament was limited to its refusal to sanction consolidations. Consequently after 1847 the railway companies, debarred from actual amalgamations, tended to introduce working agreements or pooling arrangements in order to minimize competition. In 1853, for instance, the L.N.W.R. had negotiated twenty-seven separate agreements of this nature, while in 1850 traffic from England to Scotland was pooled in fixed proportions.

Between 1860 and 1872 a number of amalgamations were effected without undue comment as time had shown that combination was not so dangerous to the public interest as had been thought. But from 1873 to 1893 public apprehensions were again roused, and in this period the State greatly increased its control over the railways and the new regulation was much more effective than the somewhat half-hearted attempts of earlier years. The immediate cause was the revival of numerous ambitious projects for amalgamation, such as that proposed between the L.N.W.R. and the

Lancashire and Yorkshire in 1872 or that of the Midland and the Glasgow and South-Western Railways. About this time, almost every railway, it was said, had projects of one kind or another for amalgamation. Chambers of Commerce, traders, and the general public became greatly alarmed about the possible dangers of monopoly, and protests poured in to Parliament and the press. In 1872 this agitation led to the appointment of a Commission to examine once more the question of amalgamation, and as a result of its report, a tribunal of experts, called the Railway and Canal Commission, was set up by the Act of 1873. The Commissioners were to enforce Cardwell's Act of 1854[3] relating to ' undue preference ' which had previously never been properly administered; they were to hear complaints about preferences; to decide whether through rates were reasonable; and to examine, and if necessary veto, schemes of amalgamations or agreements between railway companies. In addition—though in 1873 it was hardly necessary—they were to investigate all proposals by railway companies to buy up canals.

Unlike the numerous earlier Boards or Commissions, the Railway and Canal Commission was able to exert an effective control over the railways. Appointed in the first instance for only five years, the tribunal was continued till 1888, when it became a permanent body under the Railway and Canal Traffic Act of that year and was given additional powers. The Commission is still in existence, having survived the Railways Act 1921, but most of its powers have now passed to the Rates Tribunal.

In the new century, a number of working agreements were effected, a stimulus being given by rising expenditure and keen competition for traffic. The first of the new agreements was the working union formed by the South-Eastern and Chatham Companies in 1899. This was followed by an agreement between the L.N.W.R. and the Lancashire and Yorkshire Railway, while in 1908 the L.N.W.R. made another agreement with the Midland Company. A Govern-

³ See Chapter II, p. 32.

ment committee, appointed in 1909 to consider again the question of amalgamation, reported more favourably on it, and this report is indicative of the changed opinions on the problem.

### THE ADVANTAGES OF COMBINATION

It is obvious that behind the strong and continued trend towards combination which was evident throughout the nineteenth century, there must have been weighty economic advantages which provided a stimulus to agreement between highly competitive systems. Amalgamations, working agreements, and other forms of combination have, in fact, great economic and financial attractions to the participating companies, and these advantages can in turn be passed on to the public provided the monopoly thus established is suitably regulated by the Government. Combination avoids wasteful capital expenditure and enables equipment to be worked to the best advantage. Duplication of services and accommodation is avoided and unnecessary running mileage can be eliminated, while trains can be given better loads. With the same number of trains better services can be provided for the public, since the services can be spread over the day instead of being concentrated at the hours in which most traffic is expected. Unity of management and control increases efficiency and economy, especially where formerly competing companies were fairly small. The shortest routes available can be utilized and a better distribution of rolling stock and locomotives can be effected to meet fluctuations of traffic. The wastes of competition are especially great on railways with their large fixed capital and their marked susceptibility to the economic law of decreasing costs.

## CHAPTER VII

# THE RAILWAY CLEARING HOUSE

THE Railway Clearing House, or as often called in abbreviated form, the R.C.H., was established in 1842, nine railways being parties to its foundation. In 1850 the Railway Clearing Act gave it a definite legal status, enabling it to sue a debtor company in its own name. Government recognition was again extended to it in 1897 when it was re-incorporated.

Unfortunately, few records have been preserved about the details of the early work of the Clearing House, but obviously it was modelled on the Bankers' Clearing House established some seventy years earlier, and also to some extent perhaps on the example of the road clearing houses of the coaching era. The present membership of the Clearing House is seventeen, but previous to the Railways Act 1921 and the Irish Railways Act 1924 there were fifty-eight member companies. Certain steamboat companies and smaller railway companies have arrangements with the participating companies for clearing their traffic.

## THROUGH TRAFFIC

The primary object of the Clearing House was to facilitate the sending of through carriages and wagons from one railway system and to provide a method for the division of through rates among the companies concerned. Such facilities were found to be necessary at an early date, since the transference of traffic at the numerous junctions between the various companies was far too inconvenient and expensive. But this entailed difficult problems concerning the use of other company's rolling stock or the division of receipts, which came to involve ' an intolerable chaos of cross accounts, out of which spring vexatious disputes and much litigation '.[1]

The Clearing House provided a machinery for adjusting the complicated debits and credits arising out of through traffic. It also facilitated the apportionment of the Government duty on passengers carried at fares exceeding 1d. per mile (abolished 1929). Number-takers employed by the Clearing House were stationed at the various exchange points to note the number and destination of carriages, wagons, and sheets passing from one company to another. Before the introduction of the common user principle payment had to be made on a mileage basis for the use of all such stock, and if its return were delayed beyond a stipulated time a demurrage charge was also enforced. In the settlement of the various accounts, the principle of the Bankers' Clearing House was adopted, whereby only the balance of credits and debits was paid over between any two companies on the settling day.

At the present time the work of the Clearing House is divided into three departments: (1) the Secretarial Department, which consists of a General and a Mileage Section, (2) the Merchandise Department, and (3) the Coaching Department.

### THE SECRETARIAL DEPARTMENT

The General Section of this department is concerned with the administration and organization of the Clearing House. It is also responsible for the compilation and issue of various publications, such as the *General Classification of Merchandise, Specifications for Private Owner's Wagons,* and the *Coaching Arrangements Book.* A sub-section deals with expenditure and works out the results of the division

[1] D. Lardner, *Railway Economy*, p. 150.

of through rates and fares, balancing credits against debits for each company. A Distances sub-section compiles mileage tables, which form the basis for the division of through rates. This sub-section also compiles the official railway maps and the *Stations Handbook*.

### THE MILEAGE SECTION

This section compiles returns relating to wagons, carriages, and sheets which pass from one company's lines to those of another. Number-takers appointed by the Clearing House are stationed at the various junctions throughout the country in order to provide a record of such movements. A ' mileage charge ' is debited against a receiving company according to a tariff for the loan of coaching stock from the forwarding company. If the stock is not returned within the stipulated period, or by the appropriate route, a ' demurrage charge ' is debited. Goods rolling stock, and wagon sheets are now ' common user ', and only certain special wagons excluded from the common user agreement are dealt with and recorded in the same way as coaching stock. For common user wagons and sheets the principle of adjustment is that of allowing each company a certain number of wagons or sheets equal to its own stock, less an agreed quota if a forwarding company, or plus a certain quota if the company is one which normally receives more stock than it sends to other companies. Periodically, by means of a wagon census and daily records of transferences, adjustments are effected by the exchange of stock between the companies, so that each company is provided with its correct amount of stock. A penalty is imposed if wagons are not returned after advice is received from the Clearing House.

The ' Common User ' principle was adopted as a result of experience during the war years and it has proved an immense saving both in empty mileage and superintendence. Now all that has to be adjusted is the balance of wagons, whereas formerly each wagon had to be recorded and worked back direct to the junction from which it came. Companies are still entitled to a payment for the use of common user wagons passing into another company's line. For this purpose a ' journey payment ' is levied instead of a mileage charge, the rates being based on an agreed scale.

### THE MERCHANDISE DEPARTMENT

Receipts from the through carriage of merchandise are divided mainly on a mileage basis (including any ' bonus ' mileage applicable) after payments for terminal services are deducted. Returns are rendered each month from all stations showing the amount of goods traffic passing over other companies' lines. If the aggregate receipts between any two points in a month amount to less than 70s. the amount is pooled and divided out in proportion to the amounts of general heavy traffic. This method in practice works out with sufficient accuracy and has meant a big saving in clerical costs which more than balances any small loss to a particular company.

### THE COACHING DEPARTMENT

This department arranges for the division of receipts from through tickets and through traffic carried by passenger trains. Monthly returns are furnished by all stations relating to such tickets showing separately ordinary, excursion, workmen's, and season and traders' tickets. All spent tickets collected are sent up to be compared with the returns rendered by ticket-issuing offices. Except for small accounts, known as the ' Light Fund ', the receipts are divided in detail according to mileages. For sums in the ' light fund ' the division is based on a selected basic month. Special arrangements now apply to parcels since the formation of the parcels pool with the system of pre-paid stamps. After deductions for terminal services, the pool is divided out in proportion to an agreed formula.

## COMMITTEES AND CONFERENCES

The Railway Clearing House, in addition to its other functions, provides a neutral meeting ground for various committees and conferences. The committees, such as those dealing with claims, packing, labelling, and dangerous goods, can speak on behalf of the railway companies as a whole, thus securing uniformity in their regulations and conditions of carriage. The General Managers and Superintendents of the various companies meet in committee periodically at the Clearing House to discuss matters of common interest, and in this manner uniform standards have been adopted for wagons, coaching stock, wheel-box measurements, and signal appliances.

The affairs of the Clearing House are managed by a committee consisting of four representatives from each of the big four grouped companies and one each from the other companies parties to the clearing system. Before 1921 the committee consisted of one delegate from each company concerned, a two-thirds majority being necessary for any action.

## IMPORTANCE OF THE CLEARING HOUSE

The Clearing House has been of the greatest importance in facilitating the proper co-ordination of British railway traffic and in promoting the rationalization of the railway industry. As an official pamphlet in 1846 declared, ' The tendency of the clearing arrangements is to give to all the connected railways of Great Britain, as far as regards the working of through traffic, the character of one concern conducted on a uniform system '. In the last century especially the value of the Clearing House cannot be overestimated when the great problem was to give cohesion to the numerous short lengths of line, each under separate management. Its importance is at once evident if the railways are compared with the unorganized and unprogressive canals—a jumble of local systems lacking co-ordination, standardization, or facilities for through traffic. Incidentally the Clearing House must have facilitated the process of railway amalgamation since the frequent meetings of officials would tend to show the advantages of combination.[2]

[2] There is no book dealing in detail with the history and work of the Clearing House. Reference, however, may be made to an excellent article by Mr. P. H. Price on ' The Railway Clearing House ' in the Journal of the Institute of Transport, Vol. VII, 1926, pp. 328-42.

## CHAPTER VIII

# THE DEVELOPMENT OF RATES AND FARES

## EARLY RAILWAY RATES

THE earliest railway rates were tolls charged for the use of the permanent way and were based on mileage, or on a combination of mileage and tonnage. The next stage came with the adoption of steam locomotion. The Stockton and Darlington Railway, for instance, was empowered by Parliament to charge a ' locomotive toll ' in addition to the other charges when a trader made use of the company's engines. Then when it became the rule for companies to provide wagons and incidental services, they were authorized to make a charge for ' conveyance '. Parliament at first only stipulated that these charges should be ' reasonable ', and no attempt was made to fix maximum rates since it was thought that the competition of outside carriers would keep rates down. But when this competition began to dwindle, Parliament fixed maximum charges for the various locomotive and conveyance tolls. This was generally done when Private Acts were passed to incorporate new companies or to extend the powers of old companies. Three separate charges were thus authorized by Parliament, viz. (1) road tolls, (2) locomotive tolls, and (3) conveyance tolls.

In 1845 a ' maximum rate clause ' was passed by Parliament which grouped all three into a single rate somewhat less than the aggregate of the three. Thus was introduced a policy of reducing charges by statutory regulation, a policy which was continued right through the nineteenth century.

As traffic increased, the railway companies became definitely organized as common carriers and found it necessary to provide depôts, warehouses, and facilities for loading and unloading. For these services they claimed the right to charge something extra, over and above the maximum charges. The services came to be known as ' station ' and ' service terminals ' and it was only after much controversy and litigation that the companies gained their point, though Parliament required them to distinguish the charges for conveyance, terminals, and collection and delivery services.

### EARLY CLASSIFICATIONS

From the first, railway tolls and rates were based on the principle of classification of commodities, i.e. the various kinds of merchandise were placed in one of several groups or classes, each class being charged at different rates. In adopting this practice the railway companies were following the example of the canals and turnpike road trusts which had already evolved a rudimentary kind of classification.

On the early railways, or wagon-ways, the classifications were very similar to the canal schedules. The Surrey Iron Railway, authorized in 1801, charged rates of from 2d. to 6d. per ton per mile. There were four classes, charged respectively at 2d., 3d., 4d., and 6d. per mile, and 26 different commodities were mentioned by name in these groups.

The Liverpool and Manchester Railway had three sets of classifications, namely: (1) tonnage rates or tolls, mentioning 37 commodities, (2) tolls on passenger vehicles and on cattle, and (3) rates for conveyance (41 items).

These lists of commodities were true classifications since the charge was varied according to the value of the article, but the number of items in the classifications were very few compared with the developed classifications of modern times.

No attempt was made by Parliament to regulate passenger fares, or rates for the carriage of cattle, excepting the 'Cheap Trains Act' 1844, as it was thought that competition would keep these charges at a reasonable level. The statutory schedules of tolls and rates for the conveyance of goods became practically stereotyped, but, subject to the maximum being observed, the companies were free to vary their rates as they thought desirable. As time went on, the early lists comprising 40 or 50 articles divided into 5 or 6 groups were found to be quite insufficient, and the history of railway classification from 1845 to 1891 is concerned with the independent actions of the companies in evolving the more modern types of classifications.

### THE CLEARING HOUSE CLASSIFICATION

The Railway Clearing House was the instrument used to evolve a uniform and developed classification applicable to all the railway companies, at least as regards through traffic. At the outset the Clearing House Classification comprised about 300 articles; by 1852 the number of items had increased to 700; by 1864 the number was 1,300, and in 1886 some 2,700 items. There were seven separate classes, the lowest being a mineral class divided into two sub-classes ' M(A) ' and ' M(B) '. The rates for minerals applied only to minimum loads of 4 tons, loaded and unloaded by the owners. Next there came a special class ' S ' for loads of not less than 2 tons, covering transit from station to station only (called ' S to S ' traffic) as in the case of the mineral classes.

The higher classes were numbered from one to five (five being the highest) and such traffic was loaded and unloaded by the railway company, generally under cover in sheds, hence it was often designated ' shed traffic '. In many cases this traffic was collected and delivered by the railway (hence it came to be also known as ' C and D ' traffic or 'carted traffic'). The following examples will serve to illustrate the grading of commodities which was adopted:

M(A). Coal, coke, iron ore, furnace slag.

M(B). Clay, sand, chalk, bricks, pig iron.

S. Grain, flour, seeds, lead ore, rails, girders.

*Class* 1. Common vegetables, raw cotton, tallow.

*Class* 2. Mineral waters, biscuits, china in casks or crates.

*Class* 3. Cotton and linen goods, china in hampers, tea.

*Class* 4. China in boxes or cases, brooms, pine-apples.

*Class* 5. Amber, analine dyes, bismuth, clocks.

### THE RAILWAY AND CANAL TRAFFIC ACTS

In 1888 the Railway and Canal Traffic Act of that year established a new principle of maximum rates beyond which the companies were forbidden to charge, and provisions were made for a revised and uniform classification. Maximum rates were also fixed for station terminals and service terminals. The companies were required in the first place to submit to the Board of Trade a revised and uniform classification and a revised schedule of maximum charges which would take the place of the limited schedules of the then existing Acts. The rates proposed were to be considered by the Board and an opportunity given to traders and others to raise objections thereto.

The work of rate revision was a stupendous task, but for the classification the Clearing House tariff with slight modifications was eventually adopted, and in this manner the well-known schedules A, B, and C and one to five were introduced. The Act laid down that conveyance charges and terminal charges should be shown separately and that rates should 'taper' according to the distance over which the traffic was carried. For the first twenty miles a certain rate was chargeable, for the next thirty a rate somewhat less per mile, and for the next fifty an even lower rate. Formerly beyond six miles the rates had been equal per mile.

A bonus mileage was allowed on a few special sections of line which had involved great expense in construction but which gave traders the advantage of shorter routes. Thus the Severn Tunnel was allowed to count as twelve miles long and the Forth Bridge as twenty-three miles or fourteen miles in different cases. Other examples are the Tay Bridge, the Newcastle High Level Bridge, and the Peak Forest Line. Bonus mileages also apply to passenger fares, but some anomalies were permitted since certain towns (e.g. Kirkcaldy) obtained complete or partial exemptions.

Scales of charges for various types of traffic were laid down in the Act and these were divided into six parts as follow:

(1) Goods and minerals.
(2) Animals.
(3) Carriages.
(4) Exceptional rates.
(5) Perishable commodities carried by passenger trains.
(6) Small parcels by merchandise train.

In accordance with the 1888 Act, statutory maxima were embodied in a further series of thirty-five Acts of the years 1891 and 1892, the various Acts being applicable to thirty-five different railways, or groups of railways.

In this way a uniform Parliamentary Classification was introduced, and in most cases the maximum rates were reduced below their former level.

In addition to the various standard rates for the different classes numerous exceptional rates had been granted by the companies at their own discretion to attract bulk traffic to the rail, to meet competition from coasting steamers and canals or to encourage special types of traffic.

In 1893 the railway companies raised all their rates where possible to the new maxima permitted by the Acts. This they did partly because there was not time to revise all the rates and partly in order to recoup themselves for the reductions imposed by the new legislation. A storm of complaints arose and in 1894 the Railway and Canal

G

Traffic Act of that year was passed which in effect made the rates of *1892* the maximum rates where these were lower than the level permitted by the new Acts. To raise any rate above this level the railway company had to be able to show that there was an increased cost in working that particular traffic. Railway rates were thus deprived of a certain amount of elasticity and the companies henceforth became extremely careful in making reductions in existing authorized rates because they felt that there might be difficulties in restoring them to their former level should they prove uneconomical. The 1894 Act also imposed on the companies the obligation to keep at their head offices a rate book showing the rates in force on December 31, 1892.

### RATES ADVISORY COMMITTEE

Up to 1914 the position remained unchanged except that a slight modification amounting to 4 per cent. on ' exceptional rates ' was granted so that the companies might recoup themselves for increased wages after the strike settlement of 1911. During the war the railways were operated at a loss owing to the increase in prices and wages, and after the war it was found necessary to raise both rates and fares. The Act of 1919, which set up the Ministry of Transport, provided for the formation of a Rates Advisory Committee to give advice and assistance to the Minister on questions relating to railway rates. The Committee reported in the same year, and in 1920 new rates were authorized, including a 20 per cent. increase in coal traffic rates and a 60 per cent. increase in the rates for merchandise. Later a further increase in merchandise rates was sanctioned. In 1920 the Committee issued a further comprehensive report[1] which formed the basis of the provisions of Part III of the Railways Act 1921. In 1923 freight rates were reduced from 60 per cent. to 50 per cent. over pre-war levels.

[1] Cmd. 1098.

## PASSENGER FARES

On the early railways, contrary to expectations, passenger traffic was more important than goods, and in the 'forties about three-quarters of the total railway revenue was derived from passengers, while on the important trunk lines the proportion was even greater. As time went on the receipts from goods increased till in the early 'fifties they represented about half the total revenue, but since then the percentage has not increased very greatly.

Originally third-class fares were 1½d. per mile, but the accommodation was very primitive, sometimes only open trucks being provided. In 1844 the Railway Regulation Act required the railway companies to run at least one train each way over every passenger-carrying line each lawful day, stopping at all stations, and conveying third-class passengers at 1d. per mile. The average speed was not to be less than 12 m.p.h.[2] The ' Parliamentary ' trains, though the carriages had to be provided with seats and passengers protected from the weather, were tediously slow and the companies did not encourage cheap travel in any way except for a few excursions run early in the history of the railways. In 1872, however, the Midland Railway decided to admit third-class passengers to all their trains. This innovation, though at first resisted by the other companies, was gradually adopted by all the lines. A revolution in railway travel was thus introduced by the Midland, and the most striking development since then has been the remarkable growth of third-class travel. Third-class passengers are greatly in the majority and they account for the greatest bulk of railway passenger revenue.

In 1842 there were some 18,000,000 passengers, nearly all of whom travelled first class, but in 1912 passengers,

[2] The Cheap Trains Act 1883 repealed these sections of the 1844 Act, but provided that ' a due and sufficient proportion of the accommodation provided ' should be available for passengers at fares not exceeding 1d. per mile. The Act also provided for exemption from the 5 per cent. tax payable on other fares.

including season ticket holders, numbered about 1,162,000,000, and nine-tenths of these travelled third class at an average fare of ½d. per mile.   In 1914 passenger fares were practically the same as they had been for many years, though special fares and concessions were freely granted as occasion seemed to require.   The railways were not hampered in this respect as they were in the case of goods traffic by the 1894 Act or the law of undue preference.

During the war, in order to discourage unnecessary travel, tourist, excursion, and week-end ticket facilities were withdrawn in 1915.[3]   In 1917 a 50 per cent. increase was made in ordinary fares which had been kept at their pre-war level and there was also a 10 per cent. advance in season ticket rates.   In 1920 a 16⅔ per cent. increase on passenger fares was introduced, making a 75 per cent. advance on pre-war fares, and increases were also sanctioned for workmen's tickets and season tickets.

In 1921 week-end tickets were restored and in 1923 ordinary fares were reduced to a level of 50 per cent. over pre-war charges.   During the summer of 1925 most of the pre-war facilities were reintroduced, including excursion tickets, half-day tickets, and tourist tickets.

[3] Certain restrictions were also imposed on routes by which passengers might travel to destinations served by more than one route.

## CHAPTER IX

# THE RAILWAYS ACT 1921

## GOVERNMENT CONTROL DURING THE WAR

ON the outbreak of war in 1914, a ' Railway Executive Committee ', consisting of the General Managers of the principal railway companies, was set up by the Government to take over control of the railways. In this way the railways were mobilized for war purposes; troops, munitions, and other war materials were carried free of cost to the Government; railway repairs and maintenance were cut down to the minimum; and a great deal of railway material was sent overseas to the war areas. A certain amount of reorganization was also effected, such as the introduction of common user of rolling stock or inter-availability of tickets between certain common points. In return for the services rendered by the railway companies, the Government agreed to compensate them after the war for loss of revenue and for repairs and renewals postponed during the period of control. Thus to the credit of the railways, it can be said that they made no excess profits out of their country's need.

## THE RAILWAYS ACT 1921

This Act was the instrument whereby the systems were returned to their owners and compensation granted as promised by the Government. The opportunity was also utilized to readjust the relations of the railways to the State, their employees and customers, and to each other. The Act is by far the most comprehensive statute which has ever been passed to regulate British railways, and its provisions are of the greatest importance. There are six parts, each dealing with separate aspects, and nine schedules.

### PART I. REORGANIZATION OF THE RAILWAY SYSTEM

This part of the Act provided for the amalgamation of numerous independent companies into four groups, ' with a view to the reorganization and more efficient and economical working of the railway system of Great Britain '. The more important companies in each group were termed ' constituent companies ' and were to be amalgamated, i.e. stockholders and debenture-holders were to exchange their holdings for corresponding holdings in the new group. The remaining companies allotted to a group were called ' subsidiary companies ' and were to be absorbed by the purchase of their stock by the group.

In the first schedule of the Act the four groups were designated as :

(1) *The Southern Group*, comprising five constituent companies and fourteen subsidiary companies.

(2) *The Western Group*, with seven constituent and twenty-six subsidiary companies.

(3) *The North-Western, Midland, and West Scottish Group*, comprising eight constituent and twenty-seven subsidiary companies.

(4) *The North-Eastern, Eastern, and East Scottish Group*, consisting of seven constituent and twenty-six subsidiary companies.

Subsequent to the passing of the Act, the respective combinations of railways in these areas assumed the following titles : (1) *The Southern Railway*; (2) *The Great Western Railway;* (3) *The London, Midland, and Scottish Railway*; and (4) *The London and North-Eastern Railway*.

*Formation of the groups.* The constituent companies in each group were permitted to submit amalgamation schemes to the Minister of Transport on or before January 1, 1923, and these were to be examined by a ' Railways Amalgamation Tribunal ', consisting of three commissioners named in the Act, who were to hold office until the amalgamations were completed. In the event of a group failing to submit an agreed scheme, the Tribunal was empowered to frame a compulsory scheme of amalgamation.

In spite of the great difficulties inherent in the amalgamations, the work was effected with considerable rapidity, and by January 1, 1923, all but two companies—the Caledonian Railway and the Midland and South-Western Junction Railway—had come to voluntary agreements. The two outstanding mergers were settled in 1923, and the Railways Amalgamation Tribunal was dissolved in October of that year. In effecting the combinations only a very small transfer of cash was necessary, as the method generally adopted was that of a fusion of capital and the reissue of securities and shares to the stock-owners of the original companies.

In this way 120 railway companies out of a total of some 214 separate companies existing in 1921 were combined into one or other of the four big groups, and their capital represented slightly more than 90 per cent. of the total investment in the railways of the country. Some 94 companies were excluded from the combination, but of these 44 were jointly owned, or leased by two or more of the groups, or by one of the groups and an outside company, e.g. the Cheshire Lines Railway. Of the remaining 50 railway companies, seven or eight are urban or suburban lines, e.g. the Metropolitan District and the Liverpool Overhead railways; nearly 20 are narrow gauge lines, e.g. the Welsh Highland Railway (1 foot 11½ inches) and the Eskdale Railway (15 inches); a few are in reality tramways, e.g. the Mumbles Railway and the Wantage Steam Tramway; others are very small, e.g. the Corringham Light Railway (length 2¾ miles).

*Compensation.* Under Part I of the Act, provision was made for the payment of compensation to the companies for deficiencies in net receipts and in respect of repairs and renewals during the period of war control. The amount due by the Government was assessed at £60,000,000, and this sum was to be paid in two equal instalments on 31st December, 1922 and 1923. In case the companies failed to agree among themselves about the distribution of this money, powers were vested in the Amalgamation Tribunal to prepare a compulsory scheme of allocation.

### PART II. REGULATION OF RAILWAYS

This section of the Act was intended to secure reasonable facilities, to promote standardization, and to regulate any further amalgamation. The Railway and Canal Commission was entrusted with the hearing of complaints regarding facilities or services, and the Commissioners may require a railway company to afford reasonable facilities, including alterations, extensions, or improvements, costing not more than £100,000. Orders made by the Commission, however, must not prejudice the interests of the stockholders.[1]

*Standardization.* The Minister of Transport may require the companies to standardize gradually their equipment and to adopt schemes for co-operative working, or common user of rolling stock, workshops, or other facilities, unless they can satisfy the Railway and Canal Commission that the capital expenditure involved would prejudice the interests of their stockholders. Any order enforcing standardization, except by agreement with the companies concerned, must be referred to a committee consisting of representatives of each of the groups, together with three other persons selected from the panels set up under Section 23 of the Ministry of Transport Act 1919. In the past, there has been some lack of standardization on British railways owing to the great number of companies, but amalgamation has done much to promote uniformity. For example, the vacuum brake is now standard, whereas formerly there were two types of automatic brakes.

*Further amalgamation.* The Minister of Transport under Section 18 is given power to confirm agreements, which

---

[1] The Commission has decided, for example, that it is not a ' reasonable facility ' to require a railway to continue an unprofitable passenger service. (Decision July 23, 1931.)

may be entered into by any of the four grouped railways for the purchase, leasing, or working of other railways.

### PART III. RAILWAY CHARGES

*The Rates Tribunal.* A Railway Rates Tribunal was set up as a permanent body consisting of three members appointed by the Crown, one of whom must be a person experienced in commercial affairs, one a person of experience in railway business, and one—the President—an experienced lawyer. A General and a Railway Panel were also established from which two additional members may be added to the Tribunal upon application by the parties concerned, or when the Minister of Transport considers it expedient. These are nominated by the Minister, one from each panel. The General Panel consists of thirty-five persons representing trading interests, labour, railway passengers, and agriculture. The Railway Panel consists of twelve members, of whom eleven represent the Railway Companies Association and one represents other railways and light railways not parties to the Railway Companies Association.

The Rates Tribunal was entrusted with many of the powers formerly exercised by the Railway and Canal Commission, though at the same time it was given many additional powers and duties. Decisions of the Tribunal go by a majority of votes, including those of any additional members, and appeals from its decisions are only allowed on questions of law.

The jurisdiction of the Tribunal is very extensive, including the determination and adjustment of rates, fares, through rates, group rates, terminal rebates and other charges, and the adjustments of classification and conditions of packing and of carriage. It has also powers to determine the constitution and functions of local joint committees and the centres at which they may be established.[2]

[2] To these functions of the Tribunal certain other duties have been added by the Railways (Road Transport) Acts 1928 and the Local Government Act 1929.

*The new classification.*    The classification of merchandise and the number of classes was in the first place to be that recommended by the Rates Advisory Committee. Each group was required to submit to the Rates Tribunal ' a schedule of standard charges ' based on the new classification showing the various rates, fares, and other charges proposed by the group.    The various charges, according to the Eighth Schedule of the Act, were to be divided into eight parts, viz.: Part I, Rates for goods and minerals for each of the classes specified in the classification; Part II, Charges for animals; Part III, Charges for carriages; Part IV, Charges for perishable commodities by passenger train or similar service; Part V, Charges for small parcels; Part VI, Charges for merchandise of an exceptional character; Part VII, Fares and charges for passengers and their luggage, and for live-stock, carriages, parcels, or merchandise by passenger train or similar service other than those included in the previous parts; Part VIII, Tolls payable by traders.

*The Appointed Day.*    The Rates Tribunal was to consider the schedules submitted by the railway companies, and after hearing objections was to fix the charges and appoint a day when they would come into operation. Eventually this Appointed Day was fixed after protracted discussion for 1st January, 1928.    On that date, the old statutory classifications were replaced by the new classification of 21 classes, and the new regulations regarding charges were brought into operation.

The standard charges thus fixed cannot be varied by the groups without the permission of the Tribunal, either upwards or downwards, except by way of an exceptional rate or fare continued or granted under the provisions of the Act, or in respect of competitive traffic.    The Tribunal was also empowered to apply the schedule of any grouped company to any other railway excepting a light railway not connected with one of the groups.

*Exceptional Charges.*    After the Appointed Day all exceptional rates were to be cancelled except those not less than 5 per cent. below the standard rate applicable and which were continued by agreement between the railway and the traders concerned, or, failing agreement, were referred to the Tribunal for decision (Section 36). Exceptional rates not used during 1921 and 1922 were to be discontinued unless a trader could show that abnormal trade conditions were responsible for their disuse or that a similar rate to the same destination remained in operation at other stations or sidings in the same group or area. Any exceptional rate more than 40 per cent. below the standard rate chargeable had to be referred to the Rates Tribunal.

New exceptional rates may be introduced on or after the Appointed Day at the discretion of the companies, except that such rates less than 5 per cent. or more than 40 per cent. below the standard rate must receive the consent of the Tribunal (Section 37).

If the Minister of Transport considers that new exceptional rates are being granted to the prejudice of traders or so as to jeopardize the earning of the ' standard revenue ', he may refer the matter to the Rates Tribunal, which, after hearing evidence, may either revise the standard revenue of the group, or cancel, or modify all or any such exceptional rates. All new or reduced exceptional rates not coming within the purview of the Rates Tribunal must be reported to the Minister of Transport.

A trader at any time may apply to the Rates Tribunal to fix a new exceptional rate. The railway companies may not increase or cancel exceptional rates fixed by the Tribunal without permission, but they may reduce any exceptional rate so long as it is not brought more than 40 per cent. below the standard rate, in which event the consent of the Tribunal would be required. Exceptional rates not fixed by the Tribunal may be increased or cancelled by the railway company on thirty days' notice being given, during which traders have the opportunity of raising objections before the Tribunal. Exceptional rates not used during a period of two years may be cancelled by the company at its discretion.

The Minister of Transport, on representation from shipping or canal interests, may refer to the Rates Tribunal any exceptional rates so competitive with coastwise shipping or canals as to be detrimental to the public interest and inadequate having regard to the cost of affording the service. The Tribunal, after hearing evidence, may then vary or cancel any such rates (Section 39).

*Disintegration of exceptional rates.* The Tribunal, in fixing or sanctioning an exceptional rate, must determine the amounts, if any, to be included in the rate for (*a*) conveyance, (*b*) station terminals, (*c*) service terminals, and (*d*) accommodation and services rendered at private sidings. Exceptional rates granted by a railway company may similarly be disintegrated, but if a ' station to station ' rate is not so split up, it is regarded as composed of conveyance rate and terminal charges in the same proportion as those of the corresponding standard rate.   For other than ' station to station ' rates the company on request must afford information as to the proportions.

*Conditions of risk.* Where an exceptional rate is in operation under owner's risk or company's risk and the difference in liability is not insignificant, the company on request must quote a corresponding rate under the other set of conditions.   The difference between a company's and an owner's risk rate must be fairly equivalent to the amount of the risk (Section 46).

*Exceptional fares.* There are no restrictions on the grant of exceptional fares less than the standard fare provided they are reported to the Minister of Transport, who may refer the matter to the Tribunal if other users are adversely affected or if the standard revenue is thereby jeopardized.

*Circuitous routes (Section 52).* Where two places are connected by competitive routes, one of which is shorter than the other, the lower rate may be charged provided it is not ' circuitous ', i.e. longer by 30 per cent. or more than the shorter route.   Old circuitous routes were allowed to come under the shorter distance rule at the discretion

of the Rates Tribunal, but any new ' circuitous route '
brought under the rule must be reported to the Minister
of Transport, who may refer the matter to the Tribunal
for its decision.   If the distance exceeds the shorter route
or routes by 50 per cent. or more, the express consent of
the Tribunal is necessary.

Over 110,000 circuitous routes have now been approved,
and on all of these the shortest distance rate may be
charged, e.g. between Edinburgh and Peebles the same
rate may be charged by the circuitous L.M.S.R. route via
Carstairs, which is 54 miles long, as by the direct L.N.E.R.
route, which is only 27 miles.   The existence of so many
roundabout routes is a cause of delay and long transit times,
but as matters are at present no company is willing to hand
over traffic to another unless some pooling scheme is in
operation.   In the U.S.A., where distances are much
greater, the problem is a more serious one.   For example,
between Philadelphia and Pittsburg the direct route is 200
miles, but sometimes as much as 57 per cent. of the traffic
is sent by an indirect route of 700 miles.

*The standard revenue (Section 58).* The charges for
each group were to be fixed in the first instance by the
Rates Tribunal, so that, together with the other sources of
revenue, they would, ' so far as practicable, yield with
efficient and economical working and management ' an
annual net revenue (called the standard revenue) equivalent to the aggregate net revenues of the constituent and
subsidiary companies in 1913, together with (a) a sum equal
to 5 per cent. on capital expenditure forming the basis on
which interest was allowed at the end of the period during
which the railways were in the possession of the Government; and (b) an allowance for additional capital expended
so as to enhance the value of the undertaking since
January 1, 1913, and not included above; and (c) a
reasonable allowance in respect of capital expenditure (not
less than £25,000 in each case and not included in (a)) on
works enhancing the value of the undertaking, but which
had not become fully remunerative in 1913; and (d) an

allowance up to 33⅓ per cent. of any economies that might be effected through amalgamation.

If the Tribunal, when fixing the charges necessary to produce the standard revenue, finds that a company is making inadequate charges in connexion with its ancillary business, it may take into account the revenue which would have been produced if adequate charges were in operation.

At the end of the first year, after the Appointed Day, the Tribunal, as laid down in the Act, reviewed the standard and exceptional charges of each of the four companies. Thereafter, at the end of each succeeding year the Tribunal has again reviewed the position, and so far the standard revenues have not been earned, but few changes have been made in the charges since these would not have increased earnings. If there is in any year a surplus over the standard revenue, 80 per cent. of this is to go in the reduction of charges and 20 per cent. to the company. As far as practicable the Tribunal, in making modifications, are to avoid prejudicing the financial position of any other railway company.

| STANDARD AND ACTUAL NET REVENUES. | | | | |
|---|---|---|---|---|
| | L.M.S.R. | L.N.E.R. | G.W.R. | S.R. |
| Actual Net Revenue | £ | £ | £ | £ |
| 1928 | 16,270,821 | 11,277,759 | 7,057,122 | 6,394,412 |
| 1929 | 17,175,282 | 13,061,250 | 8,198,644 | 6,547,965 |
| 1930 | 13,426,290 | 11,168,749 | 6,987,146 | 6,133,927 |
| Standard Revenue | 20,326,622 | 14,787,733 | 8,312,013 | 6,631,479 |
| Allowances for additional capital Fixed in respect of 1928 | 118,232 | 44,384 | 49,054 | 90,050 |
| Fixed in respect of 1929 | 55,049 | 36,795 | 8,432 | 34,341 |
| Fixed in respect of 1930 | 75,000 | 148,644 | nil | 122,610 |

PART IV. WAGES AND CONDITIONS OF SERVICE

An elaborate system of wage councils and conciliation boards has been set up, as described in Chapter V. In the third schedule to the Act provisions were laid down safeguarding the position of existing officers and servants of the constituent or absorbed companies.

PART V. LIGHT RAILWAYS

The Act transferred the powers of the Light Railway Commissioners to the Minister of Transport. On and after the Appointed Day any light railway connecting by means of a junction or adjacent sidings with one of the four groups is entitled to make charges not exceeding those of the group, except that in calculating mileage rates each mile of a light railway is treated as if it were one mile and a quarter.

PART VI. GENERAL

All reasonable facilities for the convenient working of through traffic passing from one group to another must be provided and all inter-change facilities existing on August 1, 1914, were preserved.

*Accounts.* The accounts required under the Railway Companies (Accounts and Returns) Act 1911 must be compiled in the manner determined by the Railway Clearing House and approved by the Minister of Transport (Section 77).

*Statistics.* Every railway company is obliged to supply certain statistics and returns to the Minister of Transport subject to any variations agreed between the Minister and the Railway Companies Association. Light railways may be exempted from this obligation in whole or in part. The statistics required are enumerated in the eighth schedule of the Act and include among other returns: (i) freight receipts, tons, and ton-miles; (ii) commodity ton-miles; (iii) passenger journeys, receipts, and passenger-miles; (iv) train and engine miles; (v) loaded and empty wagon-miles, and (vi) marshalling yard statistics.

## THE WORKING OF THE ACT

The Railways Act 1921, as is well known, introduced many far-reaching changes of the greatest importance. It implied in the first place a recognition by Parliament of the advantages of amalgamation, whereas in the previous century Parliament was suspicious of combination. Further amalgamation through purchase, lease, or working, or the reduction of competition through allocation or pooling of traffic, is not forbidden under the Act provided the consent of the Minister of Transport is first obtained.[3]

*Competition between the Groups.* Competition has not been eliminated by the grouping, and rival routes still exist between many important centres, such as London-Edinburgh, London-Birmingham, and London-Exeter.[4] The groups penetrate into each other's areas both directly and indirectly by means of running powers. Thus the West Highland line belongs to the L.N.E.R. though geographically it is in the L.M.S.R. area, but on the other hand the L.M.S.R. can reach Goole, York, Lincoln, Dundee, and Aberdeen on the east coast. The grouping did not effect a geographical redistribution or consolidation of natural traffic areas because in places the division is drawn through important industrial districts, such as the Midlands or the Forth-Clyde region. ' The effect of the new statutory grouping ', said Sir William Acworth, ' is to leave the bulk of the territory of Great Britain non-com-

---

[3] The Royal Commission on Transport recommended that use should be made of this provision so that each company could confine its attention to its own area. They also recommended that joint lines should be merged into one or other of the groups. (Final Report, p. 28.)
[4] The Royal Commission on Transport recommended pooling of traffic on such routes and the interweaving of the time-tables.

petitive, but the bulk of the traffic still competitive.'[5]   It must be admitted, however, that there were considerable difficulties in allocating companies to definite regions because Britain is highly industrialized and the companies have grown up more or less haphazard, so that their lines were interlaced in all kinds of ways.   Branches could not be transferred because of financial reasons or on account of technical difficulties, such as loading gauge or signalling.   There was also a desire to amalgamate weaker lines with their stronger neighbours, and this was probably one reason why a Scottish group was not formed.[6]   Since there was no clearly marked regionalization, difficulties may arise in the future when extensions are required.

*Economies of Grouping.*   Considerable economies were expected from the grouping, but many of the estimates made in 1921 were too optimistic.   In any case savings could only have been effected slowly, since time was necessary before the previously independent systems could be consolidated or equipment standardized.   Also it was necessary to give compensation for loss of office.   Since 1921 re-organization has progressed steadily and the amalgamations have enabled the groups to introduce many economies which would otherwise have been impossible.[7] Remarkable savings have been effected in expenditure during the past few years, amounting to about £20,000,000 per annum, though not all of this can be attributed to grouping, as part has been due to the fall in the price of materials.

If there had been no grouping, the position of the numerous independent railways in the face of trade depression and road competition would have been far more

[5] *Economic Journal*, Vol. XXXIII, p. 31 (1923).
[6] At one time as many as seven groups were suggested, including a London and a Scottish group. (Ministry of Transport White Paper, Cmd. 787, 1920.) Later there was a suggestion to form two Scottish and four English groups. (Memorandum on Railways Bill, Cmd. 1292, 1921.)
[7] For examples of some of these economies see E. J. H. Lemon, *Railway Amalgamation and its Effects on the L.M.S.R. Workshops.* Journal, Institute of Transport, Vol. XI, pp. 419-34.

H

serious than it is to-day. Some of the financially weaker lines would have been driven to the verge of bankruptcy, and even lines strong in pre-war days would have been put in a very serious position by the loss of export traffic and by changes in the direction of trade. As it is, financial difficulties have been evened out to some extent by the consolidations.

*Road Transport Competition.* The growth of road transport has been a large factor in breaking down what would otherwise have been a territorial monopoly of inland transport in many districts. In 1921 the full significance of road transport development was not appreciated, and the assumption of a regulated monopoly underlies many of the provisions of the Railways Act. Much of the prodigious labour expended by the Rates Tribunal between 1921 and 1928 in framing the new classification and charges has been nullified because road transport competition and trade depression have forced a policy of reduced fares and ' exceptional rates ' on the railway companies. Since 1928 the tonnage of goods carried at ' exceptional rates ' has increased from 66·6 per cent. of the total traffic to 76·5 per cent. in 1930. The amalgamations, however, have enabled the railways to build up an extensive system of road-rail co-ordination since the passing of the Railway Road Powers Acts of 1928. If there had not previously been a large measure of rationalization within the railway industry itself, there would have been great difficulties in co-ordinating road services. One can hardly imagine what the position would have been if the 214 railway companies of the pre-grouping period had to attempt to co-ordinate with bus services organized on a totally different territorial basis.

*Criticisms of Part III.* In regard to railway charging the changes introduced by Part III of the Act are of the utmost importance. The machinery of rate regulation is now both more comprehensive and more elastic than it was under the old system, and also regulation has been extended to matters formerly unregulated, e.g. passenger fares. A code of regulations regarding conditions of carriage has been formulated, and the Rates Tribunal, in their ninth annual report, for the year 1930, were able to claim that this code has stood the test of experience since practically no litigation has arisen on these conditions. The Tribunal in 1929 decided to adopt the simplest possible form of procedure for their meetings, and this has proved most satisfactory. They have also impressed on all parties the desirability of reaching agreements on contentious matters without recourse to public hearings.

Certain criticisms, however, have been made as regards practical difficulties and limitations in the Act. There is no connexion between the decisions of the Rates Tribunal and the Wages Boards, though wages are a very important item of expenditure. It might happen that the Wages Board decided to raise wages while the Rates Tribunal, acting independently, might at the same time decide to lower the standard rates. This might happen, for example, in a year of good trade, since with larger revenues a rise in wages or an improvement in condition of service might be demanded. However, under Section 59 (4) of the Act, powers are given to the Tribunal to modify the standard charges upwards if the net revenue of a group is less than the standard revenue, and under Section 59 (2) the railway companies can demand a review of standard and exceptional charges for any year.

There is also the question as to what is to happen during periods of trade depression or trade activity. During depression it might seem that rates should be raised to make up for loss of revenue due to decreased traffic, but this would not improve matters and indeed might make the position worse, since traffic would fall off still further. This fact has been recognized in the chronic depression of the staple industries during the past few years, and actually the groups have agreed to a *reduction* in standard revenues, which has been passed on to the depressed industries—coal, iron, steel, and agriculture—in the form of lower railway rates. The Tribunal, it should be noted, is given a certain latitude in raising or lowering the standard charges under sub-sections 3 and 4 of Section 59, which introduce the clause ' unless in their opinion, owing to change of circumstances, the excess (or deficiency) is not likely to continue.'

What is to be the procedure if one of the groups fails to earn its standard revenue while the other groups are more successful?   If the rates were different for the various groups, great difficulties would arise on competitive routes. No doubt the principle applied to circuitous routes might be adopted, but this would be a very complicated procedure.   The difficulty seems to have been present in the minds of those who drafted the Act, since in Section 59, sub-section 3, the Tribunal is enjoined ' as far as practicable ' to avoid making modifications which might prejudice the financial position of any other railway company.

Complaints have also been made that the Rates Tribunal has not done as much as it might have done to encourage traders to adopt methods which would help the railways to reduce their operating expenses, e.g. demurrage charges as modified by the Tribunal have reduced the former incentive to quick clearing of wagons.   Mr. Sherrington goes further and criticizes the Act itself, for, as he points out:

> Problems concerning the elimination of traders' wagons, of grease axle-boxes on all types of wagons, or the raising of demurrage rates to increase the daily mileage of wagons were studiously avoided, yet such economies as these, though costly in capital expenditure for a few years, would have led to enormous savings at later dates.[8]

During the past few years there has been a tendency to criticize the Act for not going far enough.   Many persons advocate a fusion of the four groups into a single whole on the ground that it would mean further great economies, e.g. elimination of nearly all the work at present performed by the Clearing House, increased standardization, complete common user of wagons, further centralization and

[8] *Economics of Rail Transport in Great Britain*, Vol. I, p. 262.

specialization of workshops, and the elimination of unnecessary competitive facilities. Undoubtedly great
economies could be obtained, but the adequate control
and organization of such a huge concern would present a
very difficult problem and might increase rather than
diminish administrative costs. Further local peculiarities
or requirements might receive less attention from a highly
centralized organization. Alternatively, some of the
economies of combination would be obtainable without
complete amalgamation by pooling traffic on competitive
routes, by regrouping of competitive lines, or by the
absorption of joint lines by one or other of the groups
concerned.

## CHAPTER X

# THEORY OF RAILWAY CHARGES

THE ECONOMIC PRINCIPLES UNDERLYING RAILWAY CHARGING

In the railway industry, fixed capital charges represent a high proportion of the total cost of carriage, whereas in most other industries the ratio of capital costs to prime costs is much less. The costs of operating a railway can be divided into three groups, viz.: (1) The actual out-of-pocket expenses of working any particular traffic, e.g. loading, provision of special wagons, driver's and guard's wages, overtime, coal, etc. (2) Fixed charges, e.g. maintenance of the plant and equipment, salaries, and a large part of the wages bill. (3) Interest on capital.

In the first group the costs bear a direct relation to the amount of work done and may be described as ' direct costs ' or ' additional net costs ', since they are incurred specially in connexion with the carriage of particular traffic.[1] Though often it is an easy matter to calculate the ' additional net cost ', there are certain complications which may render the task more difficult in regard to certain types of traffic. Thus the additional net cost of running an excursion train includes not only the direct cost of fuel, wages, etc., but also any expenses which are incurred through congestion on the main line, e.g. a goods train might be delayed, thus involving overtime payments to driver, fireman, and guard. Sometimes it is necessary to extend the conception of additional net cost so as to cover not only the provision of a specially fitted wagon, or the running of a particular train, but the whole expense

[1] See C. Colson, *Cours d'Economie Politique*, Livre Sixième, pp. 19-26.

of providing a definite type of service, e.g. passenger services on a branch line. Since the war, a number of branch lines have become unremunerative, even allowing for gains from traffic fed into the main system, and there has been no option but to close down these sections to avoid a drain on the financial resources of the company. Between January 1923 and July 1931 the four groups closed 82 branches, totalling 711 miles of route to passenger traffic. The working of passenger trains on branch lines involves extra cost over and above that required for goods traffic since more staff and higher standards of signalling are required, and this additional cost has not been met by the passenger receipts. Goods traffic is still operated over most of the branches, but its cost of working is considerably less. On main lines, numerous stations have also been closed to passenger traffic for the reason that the revenue does not cover the cost of keeping them open.

As regards the second group—i.e. the fixed charges—these are largely independent of the traffic and continue month after month irrespective of traffic variations. For the most part, they are general to all kinds of traffic, whereas those in the first group are special to particular traffic. Sir William Acworth estimated that ' on the whole, a common and probably roughly accurate estimate is to say that half the total expense is fixed; half varies with the traffic '.[2] W. Z. Ripley calculated that approximately two-thirds of the total expenditure of American railways was independent of the volume of the traffic.[3] Probably these estimates are too high, especially in view of changed conditions, since they were made, but at any rate the proportion of constant costs is considerable. Dr. M. O. Lorenz (Chief Statistician, Inter-State Commerce Commission) has given the much lower figures of one-fifth to one-tenth as the proportion of constant costs.[4] In part, the large difference in the estimates may be due to variations in the time element of the calculations, since over a longer

[2] *Elements of Railway Economics*, p. 55.
[3] *Railroads*, Vol. I, Chapter II, p. 55.
[4] *Quarterly Journal of Economics*, Vol. XXX, 1915.

period certain costs which are fixed for short periods may be variable costs over the longer period of time. For example, during a period of say five or ten years, equipment, rolling stock, etc., could be adjusted to some extent to long period traffic fluctuations. It must also be remembered that costs are very susceptible to variations in mileage, and with high mileages per annum the proportion of fixed charges per mile is greatly reduced. The aim therefore should be to obtain the maximum use out of all equipment. Sometimes, for example, it might pay to run a steam rail car for three or four passengers if otherwise the unit was standing idle under steam with its crew waiting for a later service. In this case, during the few idle hours practically the whole cost would be a constant cost.

The revenue of a railway must suffice to meet both the additional net costs and the fixed costs except that for a time repairs and renewals may be held over. Unless all these costs are met the line will eventually become unworkable. Interest on capital may be postponed indefinitely without forcing a railway to close down, but if interest were not paid, it would be difficult, if not impossible, to raise any further capital which may be necessary. Shareholders would refuse ' to throw good money after bad ' and others would not be willing to invest in a non-paying concern.

### THEORETICAL PRINCIPLES WHICH DETERMINE RATES AND FARES

Rates and fares are to be regarded in economic science as the price paid for particular services. Demand, as was explained in Chapter I, extends or increases as the price is reduced, and under competitive conditions the price would be determined by the interaction of the demand and the supply. At high prices there would be a small demand, but a large supply of the service would be offered. At low prices the reverse would be the case; the demand would be great, but the supply would be small. Under competition, therefore, the price would be fixed so as to equate demand and supply.  If the price were less than this equation price, producers would be making less than normal profits, and some of them would be driven out of business or would turn their activities to other industries. This would reduce the supply and prices would rise.  If the price were above the equation price, there would be exceptional profits in the business, and new competitors would be attracted until profits fell to a normal level.  The fixation of road transport rates for goods traffic is determined by these principles, since competition is general in the industry, and the price therefore tends to be fixed by the interaction of the demand and the cost of providing the service.  Where competition is absent, however, prices are determined by monopoly principles, the main difference being that the producer has more power to regulate the supply and fix the price at which he will sell.  Generally a monopolist must fix the same price to all persons, but sometimes he can vary his prices to different individuals or groups of consumers.

Theoretically it may be assumed that a railway is a monopoly which has power to charge differential prices per ton-mile for different commodities, even between the same places and where the service is similar.  In other words, a railway need not charge uniform prices for similar services. This is the principle of differential pricing, discrimination, or ' charging what the traffic will bear '.  Differential charging may take a variety of forms and may be made possible by (a) differences in demand, (b) differences in cost, (c) future interests, (d) differences in both demand and cost, and (e) joint costs.

(a) *Discrimination due to differences in demand.*  Discrimination of this type may arise from variations in demand due to differences in value, locality, or persons.[5]

(i) *Differential prices based on value* are the most important form of discrimination according to demand, and it occurs when different charges are made for various

[5] The problems involved in place and personal discrimination will be found fully described in H. G. Brown's *Transportation Rates and their Regulation*.

commodities solely on account of differences in their value to the purchaser and irrespective of differences in costs of handling or of transport. The classifications of all railway undertakings are examples of such differentiation, and the principle has been permitted and recognized by law.

(ii) *Local discrimination.* In this form, different rates are charged according to locality. Practical examples of its application are found in the rates for circuitous routes, in group rates, and in ' short and long haul ' rates. W. Z. Ripley defines local discrimination as ' any unreasonable departure from a tariff graded in some proportion according to distance '.[6] This is not a wholly satisfactory definition, since there may be reasonable as well as unreasonable local discriminations, but it serves to emphasize the fact that local discrimination is very liable to abuse. In consequence, Governments have stringently regulated the practice. On the long haul most railways charge less per mile than on a short haul, but the difference can be justified on account of the lower cost of service per mile on the longer distance. In Britain the Railways Act 1921 expressly makes provision for circuitous route rates and for group rates.

(iii) *Personal discrimination.* By this is meant the grant of special rebates to certain individuals or concerns which are thus favoured as compared with other persons in similar circumstances. In the U.S.A. personal discriminations formerly constituted a great evil and were a big factor in building up the economic powers of certain trusts. Such discrimination, especially in the form of secret rebates, is grossly unjust, but as Ripley says, ' It is a distinctively American abuse. European countries seem never to have suffered from it to any such degree as has the United States. It is perhaps the most iniquitous, the most persistent, and until very recently the most nearly ineradicable evil connected with the great business of transportation.'[7] Previous to 1854 there were many complaints regarding personal discrimination in Great Britain, but the Law

---

[6] *Railroads,* Vol. I, p. 215.
[7] *Railroads,* Vol. I, Chapter VI, p. 189.

Courts, after the passing of Cardwell's Act in that year, strongly enforced the point that there should be no personal preferences.[8]

(iv) *Discrimination in passenger services.* Discrimination due to differences in demand may also be illustrated from passenger services. Excursion tickets, reduced rate conference tickets, golfers' tickets, or hikers' tickets, leave the bulk of the passengers unaffected, but the remainder are encouraged to travel by rail, whereas the ordinary fares might be prohibitive to them.

(b) *Discrimination due to differences in cost.* On certain sections of line, severe gradients, long tunnels, bridges, or other works may raise operating expenses far above the average, or may greatly increase the capital costs of construction. Though the mileage and service rendered were otherwise the same as on other sections, higher rates and fares would be justified. Similar principles would apply in the case of articles involving extra cost of handling, e.g. sheet glass; or requiring special vans, e.g. meat and bananas; or necessitating higher speed in transit, e.g. fresh fruit, flowers, or fish; or where the articles did not pack well, e.g. builder's ladders. The special costs of handling particular traffics are of great importance, because they determine the lower limit below which charges cannot be reduced.

(c) *Future interests.* Reduced rates or fares may be granted with the object of developing traffic. This can be practised more easily by a monopolist than by a competitive concern since the latter has no guarantee that it will reap the benefit. Governments have sometimes forced this type of discrimination on railway companies, or have introduced it on State-owned systems, e.g. to develop agriculture or as an instrument of tariff policy.

(d) *Discrimination due to both demand and cost.* An obvious example is the difference in fares between first and third class. First class traffic will bear a higher charge and the cost of handling it is greater.

[8] A. T. Hadley, *Railroad Transportation,* pp. 182-3.

(*e*) *Discrimination due to joint costs.* Joint costs arise
where two or more things are produced together but cannot
be produced separately.  Examples of such joint products
are wheat and straw, wool and mutton, or a train service
in one direction which involves a service in the other direction.  Since one necessitates the other, the rates can be
adjusted as seems best, provided in the aggregate the cost
is covered.  Professor Taussig has strongly emphasized the
importance of joint costs in railway operating, but he
pushes the conception too far when he states that it ' is
the main explanation of the classification of freight '.[9]
No doubt numerous examples of joint costs can be found
in railway operating, but passenger and goods services are
not joint products in the sense that the provision of one
implies the other.  On the contrary, as was stated earlier,
passenger services on a branch line, for example, may be
unremunerative because they involve considerable special
costs.  In general the provision of the two types of service
affords a better utilization of the fixed capital, but that
is all.

The various types of merchandise traffic also cannot
strictly be regarded as joint products.  Though some of
the cost may be common to various units of traffic, there
are usually special costs to be met in the case of the
different items, e.g. special wagons, special loading equipment, individual handling, extra haulage.  On the whole
it appears preferable to explain the theory of differential
charging, not as an application of the principle of joint
costs, but as a form of differential charging on a monopoly
or a partial monopoly basis.[10]

THE  THEORY  OF  DIFFERENTIAL  CHARGING

On a monopoly basis, economic theory shows that rates
and fares would be so adjusted that the greatest aggregate
net revenue would be obtained.  This is the well-known

[9] *Principles of Economics*, Vol. II, p. 397.
[10] Cf. A. C. Pigou, *Economics of Welfare*, Chapter XV.

principle of ' charging what the traffic will bear '.  Because so large a proportion of the costs are fixed, a railway company finds it advantageous to accept nearly all kinds of traffic which offer, provided the rate obtained is not less than the special cost involved.  Any types of traffic which could pay a higher rate would theoretically be charged up to its ability to pay.  There is ' no norm to which a particular rate ought to conform '.[11]

Under theoretical conditions the basis of rate fixing would be the difference in *place values*, because that is the underlying economic incentive to the demand for transport.[12] This difference is a measure of the value of the transport service to the user.  For example, if the price of a commodity were 18s. in A and its price in B were 15s. the maximum rail rate which could be charged would be 3s. In practice, because of complications and uncertainties, it would be impossible to equate all transport charges to differences in place values.  Moreover, frequent adjustments would be required, and quarrels with traders would be of daily occurrence.  Therefore the approximate market value of the commodity is taken as a rough guide of ability to pay.  A transport charge of £2 per ton would make a comparatively small addition to the cost of cigars or perfume, but it might be prohibitive in the case of coal or iron-ore.

In the construction of a railway tariff, the theoretical principle followed would be to fix rates for each kind of traffic so that in each case the net receipts would be a maximum, i.e. the problem is to maximize the product of the rate per unit multiplied by the number of units carried at that price.  This may be illustrated by means of a formula.  Let $p_1$ $p_2$ $p_3$—$p_n$ represent the rates charged (less any special costs involved) for $n$ different commodities, and let $q_1$ $q_2$ $q_3$—$q_n$ be the number of units of traffic carried at the corresponding rates.  Then the monopolist who aims at a maximum revenue will have to maximize the

<hr/>

[11] W. M. Acworth, *Elements of Railway Economics*, p. 80.
[12] See Chapter I, pp. 1-2.

product pq for each class of commodity. Then the sum of these individual maxima, which may be called $\Sigma$PQ, will give the aggregate maximum monopoly net revenue.[13]

It is important to notice that in each case the charge which can be made is not entirely at the discretion of the railway because the number of units carried depends upon the price charged, or, stating the same matter in the language of mathematical economics, the demand is a function of the price. If the demand for rail transport for a certain commodity is elastic, a reduction in the rate would greatly increase the number of units carried. Thus it might happen that a low rate would pay better than a high rate, since the product $pq$ would be greater and moreover the average cost per unit of traffic tends to decrease as traffic increases.

The influence of an elastic demand is illustrated in the table below, and in the example it will be seen that the railway would fix the rate of 6d. per ton-mile, since that gives the maximum revenue.

| Rate per ton-mile in pence. | Additional net cost. Supposed constant per ton-mile. | Number of units (ton-miles) carried. | Revenue in pence. |
|---|---|---|---|
| 24 | 2d. | 1,500 | 33,000 |
| 12 | 2d. | 4,000 | 40,000 |
| 6 | 2d. | 12,000 | 48,000 |
| 3 | 2d. | 25,000 | 25,000 |
| 2 | 2d. | 30,000 | nil |

On the other hand, if the demand were non-elastic, a

[13] For a full description of the economic theory relating to monopoly prices, reference should be made to the writings of the mathematical economists, e.g. A. Cournot, *Mathematical Principles of the Theory of Wealth*; A. Marshall, *Principles of Economics*, Book V, Chapter XIV; F. Y. Edgeworth, *Papers Relating to Political Economy*, Vol. I, pp. 172-91, and A. C. Pigou, *Economics of Welfare*, Chapter XV.

higher rate could be charged without a marked drop in traffic.[14]   This is illustrated in the following table:

| Rate per ton-mile in pence. | Additional net cost. Supposed constant per ton-mile. | Number of units (ton-miles) carried. | Revenue in pence. |
|---|---|---|---|
| 36 | 2d. | 500 | 17,000 |
| 24 | 2d. | 800 | 17,600 |
| 12 | 2d. | 1,000 | 10,000 |
| 6 | 2d. | 1,400 | 5,600 |
| 3 | 2d. | 1,800 | 1,800 |
| 2 | 2d. | 2,000 | nil |

So far it has been assumed for theoretical purposes that a railway has complete monopoly powers, but in practice, of course, this is far from being the position.   In the first place railway charges in every country are regulated by the State to prevent the possibility of any exploitation of monopoly power.[15]   In this country the State formerly prescribed maximum rates beyond which the companies could not charge, while since 1928 the principle of a ' standard revenue ' has been applied.   Then again, railways are regulated by the State in a variety of ways apart from limitations on their charges, e.g. soldiers, workmen, and other classes of traffic may have to be carried at unprofitable rates.   If such low-rated traffic is carried at an actual loss, the tendency would be to raise other rates to make up for the loss if these are not already at their maximum profitable level, e.g. under the ' standard revenue ' method of railway regulation.   Further, railways do not possess a full monopoly of the means of inland transport, and competition prevents the full application of monopoly principles of charging.   The rapid growth of

[14] In 1923 ordinary third-class fares were reduced from 1¾d. to 1½d. per mile, but there was a decrease in revenue of 8·5 per cent. though traffic increased by 3·4 per cent.

[15] ' Few important railway problems can be solved by reference to the abstract principles of pure monopoly; but there is no other field of economics in which problems of conditional monopoly are so numerous, so large, and so various.'—A. Marshall, *Industry and Trade*, p. 445.

road transport has given rise to severe competition, and during recent years it has even tended to break down the system of differential charging.[16]

In order to regain traffic lost to the road, the L.N.E.R. in May, 1931, with the consent of the Railway Rates Tribunal, introduced experimental exceptional rates between certain London stations and Chelmsford, Colchester, and Ipswich based on weight loaded per truck. The rates apply to all descriptions of merchandise without distinction other than that in class 21, provided it is sent in loads of two, four, or six tons per wagon. Between London and Chelmsford the ' station-to-station rates ' are 11s., 8s. 6d., and 6s. 6d. per ton respectively as against standard rates varying from 4s. 6d. to 28s. 10d. per ton. In practice the experiment applies to traffic in classes 7-20 for six and four tons per truck, and to classes 11-20 for two tons per truck, as the standard rates for classes lower than 7 and 11 respectively are less than the new exceptional rates. The operation of old exceptional rates for particular traffic between these places at levels lower than the new rates have also been continued. The new rates are definitely experimental and do not mean a complete abolition of the classification as they only apply to traffic passing in lots of two tons and upwards, whereas the bulk of the traffic goes in smaller consignments. The rates would involve actual loss to the company unless the quantity of traffic responds, and therefore in the first instance the scheme was adopted only until 30th June, 1932, when the rates are liable to be withdrawn without further notice.

---

[16] A simplification of the general railway classification has also been urged on other grounds, e.g. the average trader finds the classification difficult to understand, and a great deal of clerical work is involved.

## CHAPTER XI

# RAILWAY RATES IN PRACTICE

IN the fixation of railway rates the principle of differential charging is applied in a modified form by means of the various classifications. These are mainly based on the values of the different commodities, though other factors, such as cost of handling, speed of conveyance, or the amount sent at a time, are also taken into consideration. In practice charging according to the value of the commodities largely resolves itself into a special method of distributing overhead costs to the best advantage. On the whole the system is socially beneficial because low grade traffic would not be able to bear the average charge which would otherwise have to be imposed and the public is safeguarded from monopolistic exploitation in the rates on high grade articles by State regulation and nowadays by road competition. As it happens, low grade traffic is very important to the country as it consists mainly of ores, iron, coal, and other raw materials of industry. But in any case this low grade traffic passes in quantity and therefore the aggregate contribution of such traffic to overhead costs is very considerable, though each ton only yields a small surplus over the direct costs of carrying it. If the low rated traffic were rejected, the remaining traffic would have to meet all the expenses by itself. A. T. Hadley put the case very well. ' Charging what the traffic will bear ', he said, ' is a very different thing from charging what the traffic will *not* bear. It is a hard principle to apply intelligently; but when it is thus applied it adjusts

the burdens where they can be best borne, and develops
a vast amount of business which could not otherwise exist.'[1]

## THE MONOPOLY ELEMENT IN RAILWAY CHARGES

Though in practice the theoretical principle of charging
what the traffic will bear is considerably modified, the
possibility of enforcing a classification rests largely on the
possession of a partial and limited monopoly. If there
were no element of monopoly, the higher-priced services
would be attacked by competition and in time this would
break down the system of classification. Differential
charging is not peculiar to railways, but is to be found in
a number of other industries and professions. For example,
electricity supply undertakings charge higher rates per unit
for current supplied for light than for power. Solicitor's
fees, legal charges, death duties, water rates, and the
Income Tax are further examples of charging according
to ability to pay instead of on cost of service. Even
' picture houses ' have adopted the principles of differential
pricing since they vary their charges according to the
position of the seat and the time of the day. The direct
costs of running a show in the afternoon are small, since
the fixed capital is there in any case and the extra revenue
obtained in the afternoon makes some contribution to the
total costs. But in the evening, higher prices can be
charged since demand seems to be greater than supply
judging by the queues, i.e. a certain monopoly element is
present. Likewise the best seats are limited and therefore a higher price can be charged for them. In all the
other examples cited above there is also some degree of
monopoly present, greater or less as the case may be.

## CLASSIFICATION OF MERCHANDISE

Classifications are to be found on all railway systems,
but the most complicated and developed are the tariffs of
British and American railways. In the United States there

[1] *Railroad Transportation*, p. 76.

are three different classifications, known as the Official, the Southern, and the Western, each of which applies to a particular territory centring respectively on New York, Atlanta, and Chicago. In addition, a number of States, such as Illinois and Iowa, have enforced their own classifications for local traffic. As may be supposed, the position is extremely complicated and has been described by W. Z. Ripley as follows:

> Imagine the *Encyclopædia Britannica*, a Chicago mail-order catalogue, and a United States protective tariff law blended in a single volume, and you have a freight classification as it exists in the United States at the present time.[2]

In Britain, though the classifications are numerous and very complicated, there is much greater uniformity since the one group of classifications applies to all the railway companies. Since the Appointed Day the classifications have been divided into five sections with various sub-divisions as follow:[3]

*Section I. Classification of Goods by Merchandise Train.*
    A. General.
    B. Timber.
    C. Returned Empties.
    D. Rolling Stock running on its own wheels.
    E. Dangerous Goods.
*Section II. Classification of Live-stock by Merchandise Train.*
*Section III. Classification of Perishable Merchandise by Passenger Train or other similar service.*
*Section IV. Classification of Merchandise (other than perishable merchandise) and Live-stock by Passenger Train or other similar service.*
*Section V. Classification of Goods by Merchandise Train, Passenger Train, or similar service for purpose of insurance under the Carriers' Act 1830 as amended by subsequent Acts.*

[2] *Railroads*, Vol. I, p. 297.
[3] See also Chapter IX, p. 106.

*The General Classification of Merchandise* (Section I A above), published as a separate volume by the Railway Clearing House, is the most important and contains a list of some 6,000 commodities with their classification. This came into operation on the Appointed Day, January 1, 1928, but year by year, as new articles make their appearance or changes are approved by the Rates Tribunal, modifications are made in the classification. The classification now consists of twenty-one classes, the lowest rate being that of class 1 and the highest that of class 21.[4] In the lower classes a trader has to consign certain minimum loads at a time in order to obtain the advantage of the lowest rate for his commodity.

As examples of the classification the following have been selected from the numerous entries in the list:

Class 1. (Six ton minimum.) Ashes and cinders for road repairs; iron ore.

Class 2. (Six ton minimum.) Fire clay; broken chimney pots in bulk; unground basic slag.

Class 3. (Six ton minimum.) Tarred road-making material; stone setts and kerbs.

Class 4. (Six ton minimum.) Iron sulphate crystal in bulk or sacks; rock salt.

Class 5. (Six ton minimum.) Unground flints; gypsum stone in lumps; lead ore.

Class 6. (Six ton minimum.) Calc-spar, crude; carbon (e.o.h.p.); china clay.

Class 7. (Four ton minimum and under six tons.) Iron anvils; bath bricks.

Class 8. (Four ton minimum.) Iron bolts and nuts; sago flour; horse chestnuts.

Class 9. (Four ton minimum.) Bone ash; ground felspar; ground flints.

Class 10. (Two ton minimum.) Alum stone; clay retorts; pears (four tons).

---

[4] A special scale applies to coal and patent fuel (minimum quantity seven tons) and coke (four tons minimum).

Class 11. (Two ton minimum.)    Cider in casks or cases; sheet lead.

Class 12. Pears (less than four tons); dog biscuits.

Class 13. Limpets; iron cart wheels; wooden plant labels.

Class 14. Lead wire; scrap copper (e.o.h.p.).

Class 15. Cabbage plants; scrap pewter; laundry blue, solid.

Class 16. Bird seed, mixed; sheet glass (e.o.h.p.).

Class 17. Almanacs, unframed; india rubber substitute.

Class 18. Strawberries (e.o.h.p.); golf balls; gas-meters.

Class 19. Art tiles; beehives; cobalt.

Class 20. Fruit grown under glass; cigars; live rats in cages.

Class 21. Gold; platinum; statuary (other than bronze).

NOTE.—' E.o.h.p.' signifies ' except otherwise herein provided '.

The rates charged for each class advance by fractions of a penny per ton-mile up to class 19; class 20 is about 1d. per ton-mile dearer than class 19, while class 21 is 50 per cent. higher than class 20.

Classes 12 to 21 are applicable to consignments of any weight, though if the consignment does not exceed three hundredweight it is charged at the special scale which applies to small parcels by merchandise train. This takes the form of an additional charge varying from 4d. to 10d. per consignment over and above the authorized conveyance and terminal charges applicable. If over three hundredweight but under one ton the charge is at a rate not less than the ' smalls ' rate for three hundredweight.

As regards the other sections of the classifications relating to traffic by merchandise train, timber is given special consideration to itself under section I B as follows:

Timber (e.o.h.p.).    Class 8.
Deals, battens, and boards.    Class 9.
Planks, planed.    Class 9.
Scantlings, planed.    Class 9.

Round timber, with certain exceptions, is charged on measurement weight according to a specified formula for obtaining the cubic capacity and according to a table of the number of cubic feet to a ton, e.g. round apple wood gives 28 cubic feet to a ton. Special charges are made for loading, while unloading is only undertaken by special arrangement.

*Returned Empties.* Section I C has eight separate classes lettered A to H, e.g. Class A, Sacks and bags; Class B, Fish boxes. The smalls scale does not apply to returned empties.

*Rolling Stock* running on its own wheels is divided into two groups, (*a*) passenger train vehicles, and (*b*) other rolling stock, including locomotives, and to these special scales of charges apply.

*Dangerous Goods* are only carried by merchandise train and have a special detailed classification for themselves which is divided into (*a*) *explosives* (for the most part in classes 18 to 20 of the general classification); (*b*) *inflammable liquids*; (*c*) *dangerous, corrosive, or poisonous chemicals*, and (*d*) a *miscellaneous* group. To each of the groups special regulations as to carriage apply. The railways are not common carriers of dangerous goods.

### THE COMPILATION OF CLASS RATES

This may best be illustrated by taking the example of the classification of a commodity hitherto not specifically mentioned in the classification lists. Such an article falls into class 20, and naturally a trader who introduces a new commodity will desire, if possible, to obtain a lower classification. The trader would make an application to the Rates Tribunal, which would consider the proposal and any objections thereto. The considerations to be taken into account by the Tribunal in deciding the classification of any such article are clearly stated in the 1921 Act, which requires the Tribunal to have regard ' to value, to the bulk in proportion to weight, to the risk of damage, to the cost of handling, and to the saving in cost which may result when merchandise is forwarded in large quantities ', in addition to all other relevant circumstances. This enumeration indeed gives a good summary of the main factors which underlie the general classification of merchandise.

### EXCEPTIONAL AND SPECIAL RATES

The complexity of the British railway rate structure is greatly increased by numerous exceptional or special rates lower than the standard rate for the particular commodity. Before the Appointed Day the number of such rates entered in the ' Rate Books ' at the various stations as applicable to certain traffics has been variously estimated as between 40 and 80 millions, and a very large percentage of goods traffic and still more coal traffic was carried at charges below the standard class rates. The enlargement of the classifications from 8 to 21, together with the restrictions imposed by the 1921 Act, have somewhat reduced the number of exceptional rates, but not to the extent expected.[5] Before the war the prevalence of exceptional rates was partly due to canal and coastwise steamer competition, and in part to a desire to obtain traffic which would not be forthcoming at standard rates. Nowadays to these influences has been added that of road transport competition.

Before granting an application for an exceptional rate, the railway company must fully consider the matter, both in its legal and commercial aspects, and this involves attention to the following points:

(1) There must be no undue preference.

(2) If the traffic is passing through competitive points, the company must consult with other companies affected.

[5] See Chapter IX, pp. 106-7. Even in 1928, when the new classification first came into force, two-thirds of the charges were ' exceptional ', and the proportion since then has steadily increased.

(3) The company must determine if the traffic is to pass at owner's or company's risk.

(4) The volume and regularity of traffic between the points concerned must be considered.

(5) The weight per truck or per train which will be sent at a time must be determined.

(6) Account must be taken of road, canal, or coastwise competition.

(7) The consent of the Rates Tribunal must be obtained if the rate is less than 5 per cent. or more than 40 per cent. below the standard rate.

(8) Care must be taken that the actual rate fixed is not so low as to involve a loss instead of a profit. Since costing systems are not available, there is a real danger that some traffic may be carried at a loss.

### OTHER ELEMENTS IN RAILWAY CHARGING

Railway tariffs in the main are built up according to the value of the various commodities, but in addition other factors are also taken into account. Thus cost of service, risk, speed of conveyance, distance, and competition from other forms of transport are responsible for modifications in classification according to value.

It is frequently argued that railways ought to base their charges on the cost of the service, not on values, presumably because cost is supposed to be the usual method of fixing other prices. But as has been shown earlier in this book, it would be extremely difficult to compute the total cost of any particular service owing to the predominance of fixed capital charges and the almost inextricable relation of the costs of providing the various services. The Inter-State Commerce Commission in the U.S.A. has made many attempts to force the railways to compute costs of service, and has even laid down certain rules by which expenses may be allocated, but the results have been disappointing.

Dr. Lardner, who wrote the first book on Railway Economics, strongly emphasized the importance of determining the costs of particular traffic, and he attempted to work out various figures of cost from data obtained from the Belgian railways. ' It is not enough,' he said, ' that the tariff produce on the whole an annual balance in favour of the railway. It is indispensable that such a balance should be produced independently on each class of objects transported.'[6]

At the present time, the railway companies periodically work out the costs of selected passenger trains, but this is done on an approximate basis by allocating expenses according to averages, e.g. fuel cost is based on average consumption of the type of engine employed.

But though it may not be possible to work out the costs of all kinds of traffic, and neither desirable nor possible to base charges on cost of service, it is very important, as Dr. Lardner pointed out, to discover if particular kinds of traffic are being carried at a direct loss, i.e. at rates less than their additional net cost.

In practice, therefore, the railways endeavour as far as they can to frame their tariffs so that additional costs incurred in connexion with particular kinds of traffic will be covered. Numerous examples could be cited where cost of service in this sense becomes a factor in rate determination.

The amount of traffic sent at a time is one important factor in the problem, since small consignments require more handling, while large consignments can be carried more cheaply. Therefore in the General Classification the lowest rates (classes 1 to 6) apply only to 6 ton loads. At the other extreme, the general parcels scale, applicable to passenger train services, works out at a very high rate per ton-mile. The G.W.R., in order to encourage the use of 20 ton wagons, grants a rebate of 5 per cent. when they

[6] *Railway Economy*, Chapter XII, p. 220. This book was published in 1850. There is an earlier book by H. Fairbairn entitled *Political Economy of Railroads*, published in 1836, but the author advocates horse traction in preference to steam locomotives for goods traffic, though he suggested the building of a trunk line from Dover to Glasgow.

are used. In Canada and the U.S.A. higher charges are made for ' less than car load ' traffic (called L.C.L. traffic).

Packing is also an important factor, and thus it will be found that the same commodity may be put into different classes according to the method of packing employed, e.g. cider in casks is rated in class 11, but if sent in crates in class 16, and if in stoneware jars containing not more than 7 gallons it pays the still higher rate applicable to class 18.

Speed of conveyance is also important, since high speed and rapid deliveries involve expense. Therefore traffic by passenger train is charged at higher rates than goods by merchandise train. On account of road competition, however, the railway companies are now offering many services at passenger train speeds but at goods train rates.[7] On the Continent rates are graded as between fast and slow goods trains. The G.W.R. recently introduced a special ' Registered Transit Scheme ' or ' green arrow ' service, in which, for a small extra charge, delivery is guaranteed for a stated date and time.

Poor loading greatly increases costs, so bulky articles are charged according to a fixed minimum load per truck, i.e. 2 tons per truck for classes 1 to 11, and 1 ton per truck for higher classes. Extra charges are made for long articles and for heavy articles weighing more than 12 tons each. Still further examples of cost of service are bonus mileage, charges for dangerous goods, perishables, and round timber.

### ZONE SYSTEMS OF CHARGING

The zone system is in direct contrast to the cost of service principle because the same charge is made whatever the distance. The best illustration of its application is to be found in Post Office practice.

[7] Operating considerations may also lead to small lots being conveyed by passenger trains on branch lines.

Some advocates of the zone system would base railway charges on the average rate, or fare, expecting that what was lost on the long distances would be gained on the short. The average fare works out at about 1s. 3d. for third class passengers and 5s. 6d. for first class. No doubt zone fares based on these averages would be very attractive for long distance passengers between say Aberdeen and London or Penzance and Inverness, but they would be prohibitive for short distances. Furthermore, the increase in long distance traffic would increase working costs. Whatever the average fixed, short distance traffic would fall off or take to the road, and there could not possibly be any counterbalancing gain from long distance traffic. The truth is that the postal analogy does not hold good for main line railways. In the letter post, cost of transit is a very small part of the total expense, and terminal expenses such as collection, delivery, and sorting make up most of the cost, and these are fairly constant whatever the distance. Hence a uniform rate is not unfair. Moreover, the Post Office has a complete monopoly for the carriage of letters and it is thus protected from the competition of $\frac{1}{2}$d. or 1d. town deliveries. Also the charge of $1\frac{1}{2}$d. for a letter is comparatively small and people do not greatly mind the high rate charged proportionately for a short distance. In the parcel post, owing to the small size and number of the packages, terminal expenses are likewise a heavy proportion of the total cost, and again the charge is comparatively small, though on a tonnage basis the sixpenny postage on a 1 lb. parcel works out at £56 per ton.[8] In Hungary a zone system of charging was partially adopted in 1889, but there were fourteen zones from the outset, not one zone, and the number was increased in subsequent years until the system was abandoned as unsatisfactory.[9]

[8] Cf. W. S. Jevons, *The Railways and the State*. Reprinted in *Methods of Social Reform* (1883).
[9] A description of the Hungarian and Austrian zone experiments will be found in Clement Edwards' *Railway Nationalization*, (1898), Chapter XV.

### LIMITED APPLICATIONS OF THE ZONE PRINCIPLE

Though the zone system of charging is altogether impracticable as a general basis for rates and fares, there are nevertheless circumstances in which the system or some modification of it may be partially applied. Examples of such applications are: (1) the general parcels scale; (2) returned empties by merchandise train (14 zones); (3) milk in bottles (6 zones); (4) passenger's excess luggage (10 zones); (5) newspapers (10 zones); (6) dogs (10 zones); and (7) bicycles (10 zones).[10]

In the United States the zoning principle has been adopted in the Rocky Mountains and Pacific Coast Territory and in the Texas Common Point Experiment. Towards the end of the last century the Erie Railroad quoted a blanketed rate for milk coming into New York City from any distance. Producers near New York objected, and the Inter-State Commerce Commission ordered the blanketed rate to be split up into a number of zones. In this case the aim of the zone scale was to encourage traders to consign from more distant parts.[11]

### GROUP RATES

In a sense group rates are akin to a zoning system, since the same rate applies to several stations, ports, or collieries in certain districts. Under the Railway and Canal Traffic Act 1888 (Section 29) a railway company is permitted to group together any number of places in the same district though they may be situated at varying distances from the point of destination or departure. In determining rates, all stations or sidings in the group are treated as though they were a single station. The distances within the group must, however, not be unreasonable and undue

[10] See next Chapter.
[11] Cf. Burtt, *Railway Rates*. The author advocates the extension of zone rates, e.g. for traffic between London and Scotland.

preferences must not be created.[12]    This section was not
repealed by the Railways Act 1921, but the Rates Tribunal
was given general powers as regards group rates.    Group
rates minimize the advantages or disadvantages of certain
places, e.g. the Humber ports of Goole, Hull, Immingham,
and Grimsby are grouped, and the rates charged to any
of these ports from inland stations is the same though the
different ports are at various distances from that station.
The actual rate charged is governed by the shortest distance.    Other examples of grouping are certain collieries
in the Nottingham coalfield or goods stations in the London
area.    In Yorkshire a common rate was applied for glass
bottle traffic to stations over fifty miles distant, although
the sending stations in the group were sometimes as much
as twenty-five miles apart.[13]
    An advantage claimed for the group system is that it
minimizes the multiplication of entries in the rate books
which have to be kept at the stations concerned.

The idea of encouraging traffic from a distance also underlies the adoption of the tapering principle where rates
decrease per mile as the distance increases.    Also on the
long haul the costs of working are less as the terminal
expenses are spread over a greater mileage.    The principle
was first adopted in this country under the Act of 1888
and has been continued by the Railways Act 1921.    The
Rates Tribunal has decreed that the gradations for goods
by merchandise train shall be (a) the first 20 miles; (b) the
next 30 miles; (c) the next 50; and (d) the remainder of
the distance.    For example, goods in class 8 are charged
3·2d. per ton per mile for each of the first 20 miles, 1·9d.

12 An  undue  preference  might  be  created  either  between
members of the group or between a member and an outsider.
Grouping, however, will be upheld if it is not excessive and if
competition  and  the  convenience  of  the  district  require  it.
(Lipsett and Atkinson, *Law of Carriage by Railway*, pp. 286-7.)
13 H. Marriott, *Fixing of Rates and Fares* (1908), p. 47.

for each of the next 30 miles, 1·45d. for each of the next 50, and 1d. for the remainder of the distance. For coal, coke, and patent fuel special scales apply, one of which is given in the table below.

| *Standard rates for conveying coal, coke, and patent fuel by merchandise train in Railway Company's wagons. L.N.E.R., Scottish, and North-Eastern Areas.* | | | | | |
|---|---|---|---|---|---|
| For first 10 miles or part thereof | For next 10 miles or part thereof | For next 30 miles or part thereof | For next 50 miles or part thereof | For remainder of distance | Station terminal at either end |
| Per ton per mile | Per ton per mile | Per ton per mile | Per ton per mile | Per ton per mile | Per ton |
| 2·60d. | 2·10d. | 1·25d. | 0·85d. | 0·70d. | 5d. |

*Note.*—Minimum quantity coal and patent fuel, 7 tons; coke, 4 tons. A rebate is allowed on coal, coke, and patent fuel under the provisions of the Local Government Act 1929, amounting, at the time of writing, to 1½d. per ton and 27½ per cent. of the remainder of the carriage charges.

Tapering rates also apply to certain other kinds of traffic, such as horses and cows carried by merchandise train, carriages, and perishable articles.

Rates for short distance traffic may be charged as for 6 miles, though if the traffic passes over the lines of two or more companies the minimum is raised to 9 miles.

The imposition of separate terminal charges has the practical effect of making rates taper, since the terminal is the same whatever the distance carried. Such terminal charges are divided into (a) *Station Terminals*, which are charged for use of the station yard and placing of wagons into position for loading or unloading at either end, and vary from 3d. per ton for commodities in class 1 to 3s. 7d. for those in class 21; and (b) *Service Terminals* for loading, unloading, covering and uncovering, which apply only to traffic in classes 7 to 21.

### EQUAL MILEAGE RATES

This principle implies that the same rate is charged per mile whatever the distance and whatever the section of line. It is thus opposed to the cost of service, zone, and tapering rates systems, which clearly are not equal mileage rates. It is impossible to apply the system rigidly since traffic conditions, operating expenses, gradients, and commercial considerations vary from one part of the system to another. Acworth quoted the example of the old High Peak Railway in Derbyshire, where the load of an engine was limited to a single truck. There are still places in Scotland where loads are as low as four mineral wagons, e.g. on the Causeway-end incline and between Kipps and Rawyards. Between Queen Street station, Glasgow, and Cowlairs on the main Glasgow and Edinburgh line, the maximum unassisted passenger train load is restricted to 200 tons in the case of the largest ' Pacific ' locomotives, and falls to as little as 70 tons with small engines. ' Equal mileage rates have been found to be impracticable as a result of every inquiry which has been held on the subject of railway rates.'[14] Indeed, owing to the adoption of the tapering principle, there are, strictly considered, only a few examples of equal-mileage rates, though standard passenger fares are definitely based on mileage. Equal mileage rates are applied, however, to the following types of traffic: Caravans (1 ton, 10d. per mile; over 7 tons, 1s. 6d. per mile); corpses (1s. 6d. per mile. An exceptional scale of 1s. per mile is, however, generally applied, and there are no terminal charges); wild animals (e.g. elephants and camels, 1s. 3d. per mile); scenery, luggage, and musical instruments of theatrical companies or of music-hall artistes (if accompanied, 6d. or 1s. per truck per mile, according to size).

In practice, mileage is always taken into account to a greater or less extent in railway charging, and other things being equal, the rates or fares are based on mileage, with the one exception of single post letters, which are charged 3d. irrespective of distance. A mathematically rigid application of the principle of equal mileage rates, however, is only possible in a few cases.

[14] H. Marriott, *Fixing of Rates and Fares*, p. 51.

## OWNER'S RISK RATES

These apply to certain commodities which are easily damaged if not well packed. A reduced rate, therefore, is granted in consideration of the trader relieving the railway company from liability for damage. In the *General Classification of Merchandise* the letters ' *a* ' to ' *h* ' are inserted in italics against the classification of specific articles to indicate that Owner's Risk rates apply, having been determined by the Rates Tribunal. The reductions are on a percentage basis as follow:

| | | | | | |
|---|---|---|---|---|---|
| *a* | 2½% | *d* | 6½% | *g* | 10% |
| *b* | 3¾% | *e* | 7½% | *h* | 12½% |
| *c* | 5% | *f* | 8¾% | | |

*Examples:* Ship's ventilators, 16*a*; copper boilers, 19*b*; wooden bedsteads, 19*c*; thermometers, 20*f*; glycerine in carboys, 20*h*.

In the case of traffic carried by passenger train the Tribunal laid down, the element of risk being so small, that there was no need for owner's risk rates after the Appointed Day. With the consent of the traders concerned, however, a series of exceptional rates at owner's risk have been arranged, e.g. for milk the rate is reduced by about 10 per cent., for newspapers 20 per cent., and general parcels 30 to 40 per cent.

*Demurrage.* This is a charge enforced when company's wagons or sheets are detained by traders. A free period of two clear days is allowed for unloading exclusive of the day on which notice of arrival is given, except that for landsale coal the free period is extended to four days. For loading, four clear days are allowed for shipment coal traffic, three days for other coal traffic, and one day for other traffic. After the expiry of the free period a charge of 3s. per day is enforced for wagons (1s. 6d. for coal traffic) and 6d. per day for sheets. These charges were fixed in 1925 by the Rates Tribunal and replaced a charge which rose from 3s. to 5s. per wagon per day after the first two days following the free period. The abandonment of an increasing scale was unfortunate, since it tends to reduce the incentive to a quick release of wagons, which is very important from the point of view of efficient operating. In other countries much stricter regulations are enforced and the treatment which British traders receive is in comparison extremely generous.

*Siding Rents* are charged on private owners' wagons left on railway company's sidings amounting to 1s. 6d. per day after the lapse of three clear days from arrival.

K

## CHAPTER XII

# PASSENGER FARES AND RATES FOR TRAFFIC CARRIED BY PASSENGER TRAIN

THE conditions of passenger traffic differ in several respects from those of goods traffic. Incidental services such as invoicing, loading and unloading, collection and delivery, or transhipment are not required, though on the other hand the cost of carrying passengers is high since expensive terminal stations, elaborate safety appliances, and costly rolling stock are necessary. At the same time, costs are increased through the need for greater speeds and more frequent services.

### PASSENGER CLASSIFICATION

Classification is not so rigid and is determined not so much by the company as the passengers themselves. There are now practically only two classes in Britain, as second class has almost disappeared except on a few suburban routes and on boat trains. A similar tendency towards the reduction in the number of classes has become evident on continental railways. In pre-war Germany there were four classes and a military class, but now there are practically only two, namely, second and third class. The former is upholstered, while the third-class carriages are fitted with wooden seats. First-class accommodation is only provided on international trains.

In Britain all express trains convey third-class passengers with the exception of some boat trains on the Southern Railway. Supplements are only charged for Pullman trains which convey both first and third-class passengers and for sleeping-berths. The charge for sleeping-berths between any two stations in England or between any two stations in Scotland, including Berwick, is 15s. first class and 6s. third class. Between any station in England and any station in Scotland, including Berwick, the charge is £1 first class and 7s. third class. The sleeping-berth supplements are justified because of the extra weight per passenger which has to be hauled, but the traffic is remunerative and the results of introducing third-class sleeping accommodation have proved satisfactory from the revenue standpoint.

On the Continent it is customary to enforce supplementary fares for the use of the faster trains. Thus in Holland ' D ' or corridor express trains, ' L ' or luxe trains, and ' P ' or Pullman trains can only be used on paying certain supplements. In Belgium and France many of the best long-distance trains are restricted to passengers travelling a prescribed distance. In Germany passenger trains are classified into five types, known respectively as ' P ', ' E ', ' D ', ' FD ', and ' FFD '. The standard fares apply only to ' *Personenzuge* ', i.e. slow and branch line trains. On all other trains supplements are charged according to distance travelled and type of train used. A small supplement only is enforced for the semi-fast '*Eilzug* ' or ' E ' category trains, but higher charges are payable for the better trains, viz.: the corridor trains known as ' *Durchgang* ' or ' D ' trains; the express trains called ' *Fernschnellzuge* ' or ' FD ' trains; and the specially fast ' FFD ' trains. ' P ' and ' E ' trains convey only second and third-class passengers, ' D ' trains carry second and third, and sometimes first-class passengers, while the ' FD ' and ' FFD ' expresses have no third-class coaches.

In Britain the standard third-class fare in pre-war days was 1d. per mile, second class was generally 10 per cent. higher, and first-class fares varied from 1·58d. to 2·21d. per mile. Since 1923 standard fares have been stabilized at 2½d. per mile first class, 2d. per mile second class, and

1½d. per mile third class.[1]   This gives a ratio between first
and third-class fares of five to three.   The extra cost of
running a first-class compartment is small, and in this lies
the economic justification of providing two classes.   Even
if each compartment on the average earns only an
additional 1d. per mile the extra cost of running is more
than covered.   On certain long-distance trains, however,
there has been a definite trend towards one class travel.
As an experiment, therefore, it might be worth while to
run a few selected trains composed of third-class carriages
and one coach of the observation or parlour-car type for
which a supplement would be payable and on which all
seats would be reserved.   On these trains dead weight
could be cut down by eliminating unnecessary first-class
carriages, and there need only be one class in the dining-
cars.

| NUMBER OF PASSENGERS CARRIED ON BRITISH RAILWAYS* (EXCLUDING SEASON TICKET HOLDERS.) | | | | | |
| --- | --- | --- | --- | --- | --- |
| Year. | First Class. | Second Class. | Third Class. | Workmen. | Total. |
| 1925 | 19,497,131 | 2,773,097 | 697,833,327 | 264,739,897 | 984,843,452 |
| 1926 | 17,015,926 | 2,433,805 | 591,491,553 | 216,757,843 | 827,699,127 |
| 1927 | 17,883,440 | 2,475,497 | 645,969,986 | 236,799,497 | 903,128,420 |
| 1928 | 17,504,348 | 2,362,688 | 639,405,142 | 247,683,288 | 906,955,466 |
| 1929 | 17,244,920 | 2,217,554 | 657,288,430 | 252,110,794 | 928,861,698 |
| 1930 | 16,454,589 | 2,306,689 | 641,867,158 | 241,386,298 | 902,014,734 |

*Excludes London Tubes and Metropolitan District Railway.

## REDUCED FARES

The standard fares are by no means the usual fares, as
there is a very great variety of reduced fare tickets avail-

[1] On the Southern Railway's express boat trains, the fares per
mile are 4½d. first class, 3d. second class and 1¾d. third class.
On the same railway Ascot and Epsom race traffic is charged
3d. per mile irrespective of class.

able. The following list, though it is by no means exhaustive, will serve to illustrate the great diversity of cheap tickets now issued: season tickets; trader's tickets; tourist tickets; period and special excursion tickets; week-end, day, afternoon, and market-day tickets; cheap tickets for ramblers, golfers, anglers, fishworkers, shipwrecked mariners, and members of sports clubs; 10,000 mile first-class tickets (N.E. area, L.N.E.R.); zone tickets (Scottish suburban stations); and reduced fares for parties of eight. There are even cheap day and week-end tickets for dogs.

The fare tariffs of British railways have in consequence become exceedingly complicated, and often on the same train passengers will be found travelling between the same places at half a dozen or more different fares. Mr. D. R. Lamb, editor of *Modern Transport*, has pointed out that this multiplicity and variety of passenger bookings confuses the passenger, and ' their existence engenders the belief that in the purchase of an ordinary ticket he becomes the victim of extortion '. Mr. Lamb argues that the ' railways would benefit from a simplification of their fares system so as to make it more attractive and palatable to the general public '.[2] Many persons go further and suggest the adoption of a standard third-class fare of 1d. per mile with the abolition of cheap fares altogether. But this has been carefully considered by the companies, and they are of the opinion that they would lose considerably by the change. In 1929 the revenue from passenger traffic, other than season tickets, was £53,000,000, and of this £21,000,000 were obtained from full ordinary fares. To make reductions which would bring these fares down to the level of road transport charges would mean a large sacrifice of revenue and it is doubtful if it would be equated by additional traffic receipts. Though some degree of standardization of reduced fare bookings and the conditions under which they are issued is obviously desirable, this does not necessarily mean the abolition of the principle of differentiation which can be supported on economic

[2] Journal, Institute of Transport, Vol. X, p. 352.

grounds. The aim of the Passenger Manager is to maximize the net receipts from passenger traffic, and if he can induce people to travel who otherwise would not do so, a policy of reduced fares would be a sound proposition provided regular patrons do not transfer to the lower fares in appreciable numbers.

Once trains have been put on a route, it is to the interest of the railway company to encourage additional passengers, since the extra cost of carrying them is small. Excursion trains conveying passengers at low fares may also be profitably operated on suitable occasions, provided (a) they are well patronized, (b) that they do not deplete ordinary trains of passengers, and (c) that they do not unduly interfere with other trains by causing congestion on the line. Reduced fares may also be granted with advantage during the slack traffic periods on suburban lines. A service will probably have to be maintained in any case during these hours, and it is better that the trains should be well filled at reduced fares rather than run nearly empty.

A policy of reduced fares may be forced on a railway administration by severe competition from motor-buses, and during recent years this has, in fact, led to a great extension of the reduced fare system, so that now the average fare for all classes of passenger is only just over ¾d. per mile.

| PASSENGER JOURNEYS (PERCENTAGE OF TOTAL)* | | | |
|---|---|---|---|
| Year. | Full Fares. | Reduced Fares. | Workmen's Fares. |
| 1924 | 47·35 | 25·54 | 27·11 |
| 1925 | 42·60 | 30·42 | 26·98 |
| 1926 | 40·90 | 32·92 | 26·18 |
| 1927 | 34·24 | 39·52 | 26·24 |
| 1928 | 28·18 | 44·46 | 27·36 |
| 1929 | 23·34 | 49·49 | 27·17 |
| 1930 | 21·89 | 51·29 | 26·82 |

\* Excludes season tickets and passenger journeys on London Tubes and Metropolitan District Railway.

The principle of classification involved in the grant of reduced fares can be seen by an examination of the restrictions imposed. Those who travel for business are marked off from the pleasure traveller by various restrictions on the day and hour of travel.

In some cases reduced fares are determined by considerations other than the purely commercial since they are enforced by legal authority. Examples are the compulsory reduced fares for workmen, soldiers, naval ratings, members of the police force, and school children. In the United States, clergymen are allowed to travel at half fares and school children are also granted reduced fares. In France reduced fares are granted to disabled ex-service men and to members of large families travelling together.

### THE FIXATION OF FARES

Ordinary railway fares are based on the principle of equal mileage charges, except for occasional bonus mileages. The tapering principle is not applied in this country except in connexion with season tickets, workmen's tickets, and day and half-day excursions, because conditions are not the same as in the case of goods traffic. Incidental services, such as loading and unloading, are not involved, and as regards use of terminal stations presumably the short-distance traveller uses the railway more frequently. Tapering fares have been adopted by the Italian and Belgian railways, and in the latter country the cheap fares over long distances enable workmen to travel astonishing distances daily to their work. On the Continent the tapering system is known as the *barême belge* as it was first systematically applied by the Belgian railway administration.

The equal mileage principle is applied in Britain to week-end, period excursion, and day tickets, but the charge is less than the ordinary fare, being generally fare-and-a-third for the return journey, i.e. 1d. per mile. Tourist tickets which allow a break of journey at any station *en route* are issued at single fare and five-sixths for point to point journeys and at three-quarters of the point to point fare for circular tours. No tourist tickets are issued to London.

The zone principle has been adopted to a limited extent by tramways and urban railways. It has the advantage of simplicity and ease of collection of fares, while from the wider point of view of social economics it has the further advantage of encouraging decentralization of urban population. But though it has been applied to a small extent for local traffic, the zone system would not work where the distances traversed varied considerably.

### WORKMEN'S FARES

Under the Cheap Trains Act 1883 the railway companies were required to provide accommodation or special trains for workmen going to and from their work at reduced fares. The actual fares charged varied considerably as between different companies, and on one branch of the Great Eastern Railway before the war, a workman was conveyed a distance of 10¾ miles and back for a 2d. fare, this being the result of a special obligation imposed by a Private Act which gave powers to the company to pull down certain houses. In the north of England the usual practice was to charge single fare for the double journey and to issue weekly tickets for the sum of five single fares.

The charges at present in force where such tickets are issued have been determined by the Rates Tribunal as follows:

---

WORKMEN'S FARES. RETURN JOURNEY
(*Distance calculated on single journey mileage for the return fare*)

| | |
|---|---|
| For the first mile . . . | . 2d. |
| For the next 3 miles or part thereof . | . 1d. per mile |
| For next     6 miles or part thereof . | . ¾d. per mile |
| For next    10 miles or part thereof . | . ½d. per mile |
| For remainder of the distance . . | . ¼d. per mile |

Weekly tickets are issued at the price of six daily tickets, and tools not exceeding 60 lb. in weight may be carried free.

---

Several difficulties have arisen in connexion with workmen's fares. It has been found impossible to define a
workman other than on the basis of a person travelling
early in the morning. But this means that a builder's
foreman, a fruit salesman, or a skilled artisan can obtain
the cheap fare, but clerks or typists with lower salaries and
whose ability to pay is less, are excluded because they
happen to begin work an hour or two later. From the
social point of view, cheap workmen's fares have the advantage of enabling workers to live away from the smoky,
congested city areas. Sometimes, however, as the Royal
Commission on London Traffic pointed out, the effect has
been to crowd the population into ' suburban slums ' around
the stations from which such fares are available. When
full train loads are obtained, the cheap fares are economically justified, but in some cases the revenue obtained does
not cover the direct costs of providing the service. Reduction in the general hours of labour since the last century
have increased the difficulty of fitting workmen's trains
into the time-tables as these trains now overlap with other
traffic. Cheap workmen's fares are issued in a number of
other countries, though not in the U.S.A.

## SEASON TICKETS

Season tickets or contract tickets are issued to passengers
desiring to make frequent journeys between the same places.
The tickets are not transferable, and the Rates Tribunal
laid down that they should be issued for periods of one,
three, six, and twelve months. In actual practice season
tickets are issued for one week or two weeks (occasionally
three weeks) and for any period over one month. A
tapered charge is imposed which varies according to the
mileage. Since the Appointed Day, uniform scales of
charges have been adopted throughout the country, except
that in a few districts where charges were formerly much
below the average the price has not been raised to the
full extent.

Season ticket traffic offers the advantages of being

definitely calculable and of securing constant patron-
age of trains, whereas otherwise passengers might sometimes travel by 'bus or tram.  British railways obtain some
profit from their season ticket holders, but in America and
France the low charges imposed have involved the railways in loss instead of profit.  In both of these countries
political and local interests have prevented the companies
from raising the charges to an economic level.

| NUMBER OF SEASON TICKET HOLDERS* | | | | |
|---|---|---|---|---|
| Year | First Class | Second Class | Third Class | Total |
| 1925 | 115,214 | 48,748 | 619,072 | 783,034 |
| 1926 | 102,920 | 45,357 | 572,964 | 721,241 |
| 1927 | 97,559 | 44,433 | 579,137 | 721,129 |
| 1928 | 90,548 | 44,158 | 570,277 | 704,983 |
| 1929 | 86,131 | 43,329 | 568,549 | 698,009 |
| 1930 | 80,615 | 42,098 | 570,539 | 693,252 |

* Season tickets available for less than twelve months
equated to equivalent number of annual tickets.  Excludes
London Tubes and Metropolitan District Railway.

On Scottish suburban lines cheap weekly ' zone tickets ',
as they are called, are issued which are available for any
number of journeys between any stations in the respective
zone.

TRADERS' TICKETS

Cheap season tickets are issued to traders who consign
or receive merchandise traffic by the railway amounting to
not less than £300 during the twelve months preceding
the application.  Additional tickets are obtainable in
respect of each further £300 of traffic.  The idea underlying the issue of such tickets is that they will help the
trader in his business and encourage him to consign by
rail, but they are more helpful to the larger trader than
the smaller and are liable to abuse.  Before the Appointed
Day the scale of charges was 42 per cent. below the ordinary
season ticket rate, but the Rates Tribunal decided in favour

of a fare 25 per cent. below ordinary season ticket rates. Since then larger reductions have been granted. In 1929, in order to meet the requirements of traders who desired to travel about the country and not merely between definite points, books of vouchers were introduced covering 10,000 miles of rail travel at reduced rates. The books are issued through the Railway Clearing House on the same conditions as traders' tickets at a charge of £50 for third class and £80 first class. This works out at a reduction of 20 per cent. below ordinary fares for third class and about 24 per cent. for first class. The vouchers may be used by any member of the firm's staff travelling on business, and the privilege has also been extended to representatives of civic authorities and the Post Office when travelling on business.

### PASSENGER'S LUGGAGE

British railways allow passengers a generous free allowance of luggage which amounts to 150 lb. first class, 120 lb. second class, and 100 lb. third class. On three or four branch lines, such as that between Wisbech and Upwell,[3] the free allowance is restricted to 28 lb. In contrast to British practice continental railways allow a much smaller free allowance.

Excess luggage is charged at defined rates per pound according to a zone scale, varying from $\frac{1}{4}$d. per lb. for distances not exceeding 15 miles, to $1\frac{3}{8}$d. per lb. for any distance exceeding 300 miles, there being 10 zones. Passengers are not allowed to hand out or take in luggage at intermediate stations *en route*, and only ordinary personal effects are allowed as luggage. Thus books for holiday reading would be regarded as personal luggage, but not so a bicycle or a canary. In certain circumstances other articles may be taken as if they were personal effects, e.g. eggs, butter, or groceries purchased for domestic use (60 lb. third class and 120 first class). Traders, market

[3] This particular line serves an intensely cultivated agricultural district in the eastern counties, and for the greater part of its length it runs unfenced alongside the public highway. Two specially constructed ' Sentinel ' locomotives are employed.

gardeners, and hucksters can take 60 lb. of hardware, fruit, flowers, vegetables, plants, fish, etc. Commercial travellers, actors, and lecturers may take articles for business or professional use up to 3 cwt. first class and 1½ cwt. third class. Commercial travellers are permitted to take bicycle parts, but not a whole machine in parts. There is also an increased free minimum and a reduced excess scale for luggage accompanying emigrants, fish workers, shipwrecked mariners, and ships' crews. In other countries passengers' luggage is ' registered ', i.e. handed over to the officials in return for a check. The passenger is saved the worry of looking after his luggage, but he has to be at the station earlier and may have to wait at his destination until the luggage is sorted out. To the railway company the system gives the advantages of better loading in vans, bulk hand-ling, and affords a better check on excess luggage.

Passengers may send their luggage in advance (called P.L.A.) for a charge of 2s., including collection and delivery. If collected only (C.L.) or delivered only (D.L.) the charge is 1s. These services are convenient for passengers who are thereby relieved of worry and save taxi-fares, tips, etc. The railway gains since luggage can often be conveyed by less important trains and delays may be reduced at junctions and stations. Additional staff may have to be employed during the holiday season, but this expense should be covered by the receipts.

In the north of Scotland shop parcels may be sent to the station and are kept without charge till the passenger calls. In other districts shop parcels tickets are issued in bundles of thirty to shopkeepers at a price of 5s.

### MERCHANDISE BY PASSENGER TRAIN OR OTHER SIMILAR SERVICE

The Rates Tribunal has established various scales of charges for merchandise carried by passenger train or similar services. These are contained in Part IV of the ' schedule of standard charges ' and are divided into two divisions. In Division I, Section A relates to milk in cans, churns, or butts, and Section B to milk in bottles in cases. These are known to railwaymen as MA and MB. The rates in both sections are blanketed into six zones, as is shown in the example below.

| MILK IN CANS, CHURNS, OR BUTTS. RATE PER IMPERIAL GALLON. | | | | | | |
|---|---|---|---|---|---|---|
| Zone | Up to 20 miles | Over 20 up to 50 miles | Over 50 up to 75 miles | Over 75 up to 100 miles | Over 100 up to 150 miles | Over 150 miles |
| Charge | 0·20d. | 0·60d. | 0·87d. | 1·00d. | 1·25d. | 1·60d. |

Minimum charge as for 12 gallons. Station and service terminals together total 7½d. per can, churn, or butt.

These are standard rates, but in practice practically all milk in cans, churns, or butts is carried at an Owners' Risk Exceptional Scale of Rates.

Division II is divided into four sections, which cover various kinds of fish, vegetables, and other foodstuffs. These are known respectively as Section 1 (or by railwaymen for convenience of reference as P1), including, for example, eels, cockles, and ice; Section 2 (or P2) e.g. herbs, peas, and watercress; Section 3 (or P3) e.g. asparagus, melons, mushrooms, and tomatoes; Section 4 (or P4) e.g. cheese, salmon, trout, oysters, meat, flowers. Zone scales of charges as shown on p. 158 are in force, though the bulk of the traffic is carried at exceptional rates.

Merchandise by passenger train other than perishables is divided into thirteen groups, to each of which specific scales of charges apply, known as G1, G2, G3, etc. The various groups are set out below.

Group 1. General parcels.

Group 2. Merchandise of a frail nature or bulky in proportion to weight. In general this is charged 50 per cent. above Group 1.

Group 3. Newspapers.
Group 4. Returned empties.
Group 5. Live-stock, divided into 5 sections.
Group 6. Bicycles, invalid chairs, perambulators, etc.
Half rate is charged when accompanied by a passenger.
There is a lower rate at owner's risk for unaccompanied articles in this group.
Group 7. Loaded van traffic in trucks.
Group 8. Carriages, motor-cars, etc.

### DIVISION II.
### PERISHABLE MERCHANDISE BY PASSENGER TRAIN.
*Rate for conveyance per cwt. per mile.*

|  | For the first 10 miles | For the next 10 miles | For the next 30 miles | For the next 50 miles | For remainder of distance |
|---|---|---|---|---|---|
| Section 1 ... ... | 0·60d. | 0·55d. | 0·40d. | 0·25d. | 0·24d. |
| Section 2 ... ... | 0·65d. | 0·60d. | 0·45d. | 0·28d. | 0·26d. |
| Section 3 ... ... | 0·80d. | 0·75d. | 0·55d. | 0·30d. | 0·28d. |
| Section 4 ... ... | 0·95d. | 0·90d. | 0·65d. | 0·35d. | 0·30d. |

Station terminal at each end 1·125d. per cwt.

Service terminals, sections 1 and 2: loading, 0·75d. per cwt.; unloading, 0·75d. per cwt.

Service terminals, sections 3 and 4: loading, 1·125d. per cwt.; unloading, 1·125d. per cwt.

Group 9. Caravans, showmen's vans, etc.
Group 10. Corpses.
Group 11. Railway vehicles running on their own wheels.
Group 12. Theatrical companies' luggage, scenery, and instruments.
Group 13. Single post letters.
Exceptional scales apply at owner's risk to traffic in all the groups except Groups 11 and 13 and certain types of

traffic in Groups 4 and 5. The exceptional scales are designated by adding the letter X to the number, e.g. G3X, and these in many cases are now more usual in practice than the ordinary scale. Indeed the bulk of the revenue from passenger train merchandise traffic is carried under owner's risk scales or at owner's risk exceptional rates, which are less than the standard rates.

A special scale of charges also applies for the insurance of merchandise enumerated in the Carriers' Act, as amended by subsequent legislation whether such traffic is carried by merchandise or passenger train.

### GENERAL PARCELS

The rates for general parcels by passenger train are blanketed into ten zones, the first for any distance up to fifteen miles, and the tenth for distances over three hundred miles. Thus the whole of Scotland is in effect blanketed into one zone for parcels traffic from London or the south of England. In the following table, examples are given for each of the zones, though actually the scale is graduated for each increase of one pound in weight.

| EXAMPLES OF PARCELS SCALE BY PASSENGER TRAIN | | | | |
|---|---|---|---|---|
| Mileage zones | Weight in lb. | | | |
| | 1 lb. | 10 lb. | 56 lb. | 112 lb. |
| | s. d. | s. d. | s. d. | s. d. |
| Up to 15 miles | 0 7 | 0 10 | 1 7 | 2 6 |
| 15 to 30 miles | 0 7 | 0 11 | 2 4 | 3 11 |
| 30 to 50 miles | 0 8 | 1 3 | 3 6 | 6 0 |
| 50 to 75 miles | 0 8 | 1 5 | 4 3 | 7 9 |
| 75 to 100 miles | 0 8 | 1 5 | 4 11 | 9 1 |
| 100 to 150 miles | 0 9 | 1 5 | 5 9 | 10 10 |
| 150 to 200 miles | 0 9 | 1 5 | 6 6 | 12 6 |
| 200 to 250 miles | 0 9 | 1 5 | 7 0 | 13 9 |
| 250 to 300 miles | 0 9 | 1 5 | 7 5 | 14 7 |
| Over 300 miles | 0 9 | 1 5 | 7 7 | 15 0 |

The zone system as applied to general parcels traffic encourages traffic over long distances and has the great advantage of simplicity. It is combined with a stamp system of prepayment, and there is a universal parcels pool in operation between the four groups. The pool is worked on a fixed percentage basis for all parcels transferred from one company to another during transit, certain terminal charges being allowed to the company which performs these services. The stamp system and the parcels pool have greatly simplified the clerical and accounting work involved and have saved a good deal of expense.

### POST OFFICE SERVICES

Under various statutes the railways are bound to carry mails on their trains and may be compelled to run trains at times and speeds to suit the requirements of the Post Office. In practice these compulsory powers are not used and the mail service is regulated by special contracts between the Postmaster-General and the various railway companies. The Secretary to the Post Office, Sir Evelyn Murray, in describing the work of his department, has paid a high tribute to the efficiency of the railway mail services. ' The postal service,' he says, ' is ultimately dependent upon rail transport, and from the Post Office standpoint the train service provided by the British railway system is extremely good.'[4]

Originally the railway companies were paid for the carriage of Post Office parcels in proportion to the postage receipts, and this was fixed at 55 per cent. After the war the companies agreed to accept 40 per cent. of the higher postal rates then enforced, and this settlement was confirmed by statute. The money is paid over to the Railway Clearing House and then divided out among the railway companies according to proportions agreed between them. At present the average postage per parcel is about 9d., and of this the companies receive somewhat less than $3\frac{1}{2}$d.,

---

[4] *The Post Office*, p. 39.

the remainder being required to cover the Post Office's terminal costs of delivery, collection, and sorting.

For the carriage of letter mails, special contracts are made which provide as a rule for the carriage of mails on all trains of the company's system, for the provision of travelling post offices, and for the running of Post Office ' controlled trains ', according to prearranged schedules. Payments are made to each company, built up of sums for actual conveyance, the running of ' controlled trains ', and a number of miscellaneous services.

## CHAPTER XIII

# ECONOMICS OF RAILWAY WORKING

## ECONOMICS OF TRAIN SPEEDS

A GREAT deal of misinformed criticism exists in regard to train speeds. It is true that speeds up to 100 miles per hour are not physically impossible and have actually been obtained on experimental runs, but such very high speeds can only be achieved under exceptionally favourable conditions. Actually there are comparatively few trains in the world which average much over 60 m.p.h. There is an economic limit to the speed of a railway train because after a certain speed is reached, the cost of raising the speed by a few extra miles per hour increases out of proportion to the gain effected. In ordinary service conditions, average speed is reduced by station stops, curves, gradients, junctions, and local restrictions such as those over certain bridges or in mining areas. Moreover, punctuality is just as important as speed, and therefore a margin must be allowed for bad weather or other contingencies. During the last eighty years the weight of trains has greatly increased, and this has offset the greater tractive power of modern locomotives. Eighty years ago loads seldom exceeded 100 tons, but at the present time loads of 500 tons are hauled by a single locomotive. When all round average train speeds are raised, however, the available equipment can be utilized to better advantage owing to the increased mileage of rolling stock and the greater line capacity, and this must be set against the cost of increasing train speeds.

The fastest daily run on British railways, and incidentally

in the world, is the 3.45 p.m. Swindon to Paddington
train, which covers the 77·3 miles in 67 minutes, giving an
average start-to-stop speed of 69·2 m.p.h.  This train was
re-timed on September 14, 1931, and the average speed
was then increased from 66·3 m.p.h. to the present level.
Services at 60 m.p.h. or more are also regularly operated
between Paddington and Bath, Darlington and York,
Leicester and Nottingham, Birmingham and Coventry,
Rugby and Brackley, and Rugby and Leicester. Numerous
trains are run at speeds between 55 m.p.h. and 60 m.p.h.,
and on the whole, British train speeds compare very
favourably with those of other countries.  Since 1914 there
has been considerable improvement, as in that year there
were only four British trains booked at over 60 m.p.h.,
the fastest being that between Darlington and York
(61·7 m.p.h.).  Outside of Great Britain the fastest trains
are to be found in Canada, France, and the United States.
In 1931 many services were accelerated in Canada,
including the ' Royal York ' express operated by the
Canadian Pacific Railway between Montreal and Smith's
Falls (124 miles) from start to stop at 67·3 m.p.h in one
direction and 68·9 m.p.h. in the other.  During the same
year services were also improved in France, and the
95¼ miles from Paris to St. Quentin were covered in 88
minutes, giving an average of 64·8 m.p.h., while from
Bordeaux to Dax (91·8 miles) an electric service averaged
61·9 m.p.h.  In the United States, before the war, the
Atlantic City trains held the world's record, but during the
war their speed was reduced and has not since been
restored to the old levels.  A large number of other
schedules, however, have been raised to 60 m.p.h. or over,
especially for trains operating between Jersey City and
Philadelphia.
    Since 1927 there have been important increases in the
length of non-stop runs in Britain, and these, during the
summer months, now include the longest non-stop runs
in the world, viz., between King's Cross and Edinburgh
(392·7 miles), Euston and Carlisle (301 miles), and

Paddington and Plymouth (225·7 miles). Speed, however, was not increased on the London to Scotland trains when non-stop running was introduced, and the average speed of these trains is somewhat below 50 m.p.h. In the winter months the longest non-stop run is that of the ' Merseyside Express ' (189·7 miles). In France there are a considerable number of long non-stop runs, including Paris to Nancy (219 miles) and Paris to Brussels (192½ miles). Provided sufficient traffic can be obtained, there are certain economies in running non-stopping trains, since maximum speed need not be so high and the cost of stopping such trains, which varies from 3s. to 6s. a time, is eliminated.

The Royal Commission on Transport criticized British railways for not accelerating their services.[1] ' It seems to us,' they said, ' that if the railways desire to prevent further losses in passenger traffic, their schedules should be thoroughly overhauled and the whole of the services should be speeded up and made more convenient to the travelling public.' No doubt there is still room for improvements on certain main line routes, but when the Commission stated that ' there has been practically no improvement in locomotive speed in this country during the past eighty years ' their criticism was wide of the mark, as reference to old time-tables would show. Average speeds have been considerably raised, though in the past occasional runs at high speed with very light trains have been recorded. The Commission, however, is on surer ground in criticizing the slowness of cross-country travel, and here there would seem to be definite room for improvement. In the United States, trains on services of this nature have recently been considerably accelerated, and now that more powerful locomotives are available for fast intermediate work, there are hopes that the same may be accomplished in this country. Road competition has made some such acceleration a definite necessity, if traffic is to be retained. Speed, together with safety, is the great

[1] *Final Report*, pp. 37-8. 1931.

advantage possessed by the railway over its rival, and this advantage will require to be exploited to the maximum. That there is a demand for speed is apparent from the fact that the fastest trains are the best patronized. Fast trains are a good advertisement for any railway.

Considerable developments have taken place during recent years in the acceleration of goods trains with the object of countering road transport competition. Express goods trains can be operated economically with comparatively moderate loads if the speed is above the average, as this increases the ' wagon-miles per train-engine-hour '. Thus an express braked goods train of thirty loaded wagons, carrying merchandise at an average speed of, say, 35 to 40 m.p.h., should be a paying proposition.

## FREQUENCY OF SERVICE

Passenger services must be provided at reasonable intervals, but the actual frequency will depend on the length of the journey. For short distances, especially in urban areas, an intensive service is essential. For moderate distances of from 20 to 50 miles an hourly service is generally sufficient, while for long journeys over 100 miles four or five services per day at well-arranged intervals should be ample. The actual times and distribution of the services operated must be arranged to suit the public demand. This is determined on short distances by office, factory, shop, and theatre hours, etc. On medium distances a general guide is afforded by fitting trains in between ordinary meal hours, though connexions at junctions have also to be studied. On long runs the services generally fall into morning, night, or afternoon divisions, but in timing night trains it is necessary to arrange that passengers do not arrive in the very early hours of the morning. Duplication of services on competitive routes at the same hours—e.g. between London and Edinburgh or London and Birmingham—ought to be avoided. Probably ' rationalization ' of such services by spreading them over the day could only be obtained through a traffic pooling scheme, but if it were done the public would benefit and the companies would not be involved in any extra expense.

The rational method of time-tabling passenger trains is that based on time intervals, e.g. every five minutes, quarter hour, or longer interval, according to the traffic requirements. Time interval services are worked on the London Underground railways and on the electric train services around Newcastle, but since the main line working time-tables are the product of a slow evolution to meet growing traffic requirements, the extensive re-timings necessary to achieve interval services on main lines would be a stupendous task.

### INTENSIVE PASSENGER SERVICES

The possibility of providing intensive services in urban and suburban districts where such are required depends on the line capacity and the actual line occupation. Probably in these districts the line occupation will already be up to the track capacity, so that any increase in the services would necessitate the expenditure of large amounts of capital. The possible methods of increasing the density of trains include, among others of less importance, (1) increase of train speeds, e.g. by use of specially designed engines; (2) improved signalling, e.g. three or four position signals; (3) quicker platforming of trains and more rapid release of train engines at the terminus, and (4) electrification. But all of these methods are expensive and would only be justified if traffic were very heavy. Generally, electric operation is found essential in the end, though the L.N.E.R. has been able to provide a very dense service with steam operation on certain London suburban services from Liverpool Street Station.

On the London Underground Railways the operation of intensive passenger services has been reduced to a fine art. The electric trains have very rapid acceleration and great braking power, and this, in conjunction with the adoption of an automatic signalling system specially laid out to increase track capacity, has enabled a maximum number of trains per track to be operated. Speeding up has also been effected by the ' skip stop ' system whereby alternate trains pass each alternate station without stopping. In this way as many as forty-three trains per hour can be operated on one road.[2]

### STEAM RAIL CARS

In sparsely populated districts or in areas of light traffic the great disadvantage of the railway compared with motor-bus services has been the difficulty and expense of providing anything like so frequent a service. Roughly speaking, a bus can be operated (thirty-two seats) at an average all-in cost of 1s. or slightly less per bus mile, and of this about 9d. would represent working costs. A small train such as is run on branch lines would involve working costs of from 1s. 6d. to 2s. per train mile even under favourable conditions. In such circumstances there appear to be distinct possibilities in the operation of steam rail cars. In the Sentinel-Cammell type high-pressure boilers (300 lb. per square inch) and six-cylinder engines are fitted. They are light in weight, the axle load being under twelve tons, and they can be operated at low costs. Indeed, for the 100 h.p. type which seats sixty passengers the working cost, including maintenance, depreciation, and interest, has been found to average 11·31d. per mile on a British railway, and figures as low as 6d. per mile have been obtained in Spain and Ceylon. Owing to the higher capacity, this gives a lower operating cost per *seat-mile* in favour of the rail car as compared with a single-deck motor-bus. On branch lines station staffs might be reduced when rail cars are employed, since tickets might be issued by a conductor, thus reducing the incidence of labour costs per passenger more nearly to the level of motor-bus opera-

[2] Cf. J. P. Thomas, *Handling London's Underground Traffic*.

tion. The average speed of the rail car is high, except on gradients, when they are at some disadvantage as compared with ordinary steam trains. Rail cars in certain districts might be found useful in supplementing the ordinary train services or in developing traffic by increasing the frequency of service. They are also well suited to working into terminal stations since they can be driven from either end.

Experiments are also being carried out with small steam locomotives, and these would appear suitable for small goods trains, shunting, or ' road van ' services. For example, 100 h.p. Sentinel shunting engines, worked by one engineman, assisted where necessary by a shunter, are used by the L.N.E.R. as auxiliaries to regular pick-up trains or for shunting light traffic. In Germany light freight trains or diesel-engined freight wagons have been employed with success on ' *leig* ' or road van services.

### PRIVATE OWNER'S WAGONS

There are over 630,000 privately owned wagons in Great Britain, and of these practically 90 per cent. are utilized for the conveyance of coal. The balance of 10 per cent. represents for the most part special types of wagons, e.g. oil tankers, ore hopper wagons, and yeast vans, and these can seldom be utilized to convey general merchandise on return journeys.

Coal and coke wagons belong to over 5,000 owners, though about one-third are the property of wagon-hiring firms. Many of them are used in well-defined areas and do not, therefore, as is sometimes supposed, have to be hauled back empty over hundreds of miles. The average haul for coal traffic over the country as a whole is under 50 miles; in South Wales coal export hauls average only 21 miles; in Fife about 20 miles; in the Lothians 12 miles, and in Lanark 30 miles. Occasionally return loads of pit props or other materials are available, but in any case coal wagons are unsuitable for certain kinds of traffic, e.g. flour or cabbages, and they might, in such circumstances, have to be returned empty irrespective of ownership.

Nevertheless the private owner's wagons are a cause of much empty running, and expensive shunting operations are necessary to sort them out for their respective collieries. According to Sir Ralph Wedgwood, some 9,000,000 'engine-hours' are expended annually in shunting coal wagons, and of this over 3,500,000 are incurred in connexion with empty wagons. But not only have private owner's wagons to be returned at once by the direct route, they are also often of small capacity, thus increasing the ratio of dead weight to paying load. The Royal Commission on the Coal Industry pointed out in 1926 that they were generally of 8, 10, or 12 tons capacity, and that as many as 57 different types were in use. Since then there has been some advance in standardization, and now only two sizes of wagons—10 and 12 tons respectively—are being built. The older wagons are often weakly constructed and thus place a limit on train loads, while their prevalence also causes congestion in yards and disorganizes train services.

Private owners, however, cling very tenaciously to their prescriptive rights. Their case rests mainly on the assurance which ownership gives of having a sufficient supply available at all times, even during busy periods. In the case of a colliery the wagons can be kept ready waiting under load to be sent away as required or used to store coal. In other trades there is the publicity value of the stock and the vehicles can be fitted specially to suit the needs of the trader's traffic.

In 1929 the Standing Committee on Mineral Transport, which was set up on the recommendation of the Coal Commission, reported that the present system of ownership of mineral wagons was defective and that eventually the railways might take over such wagons with advantage to the community, but at present they thought that this was not advisable or practicable. They recommended that immediate steps should be taken to form pools containing not less than 3,000 wagons except in special circumstances, and that after a certain date all privately-owned mineral wagons should be allocated to recognized wagon pools.

They considered that pooling would reduce shunting and other costs, since there would not be the same need to separate out wagons for individual collieries, but this limited ' common user ' would of course only secure a partial economy. In 1929, out of 338,000 colliery-owned wagons about 150,000, or 45 per cent., were being worked in 43 pools, comprising from 300 to 12,500 wagons in each group.[3]

### HIGH CAPACITY WAGONS

In 1930 British railways owned some 690,000 merchandise and mineral wagons as compared with the 630,000 in private ownership. The total tonnage capacity of companies' stock was over 7,500,000 tons (excluding brake vans), giving an average capacity of 11·301 tons.[4] As is shown in the following table, there has been a steady rise in average capacity since 1922 owing to the adoption of standard 12-ton wagons.

| AVERAGE WAGON CAPACITY IN TONS | | | | |
|---|---|---|---|---|
| 1922 | 1925 | 1927 | 1929 | 1930 |
| 10·35 | 10·75 | 10·99 | 11·20 | 11·301 |

Twelve-ton wagons have increased in number from 154,118 in 1925 to 252,677 in 1930, while those 20 tons or more in capacity have grown from 25,008 in 1925 to 29,018 in 1930.

[3] Cf. Report of Royal Commission on the Coal Industry, Cmd. 2600 (1926); Report of Standing Committee on Mineral Transport, Cmd. 3420 (1929); Report of Royal Commission on Transport, Cmd. 3751 (1931); T. B. Hare, *Practical Railway Operating*, pp. 134-141.

[4] In other countries the average capacity is a good deal higher, e.g. Belgium, 15½ tons; Germany, 16 tons; the U.S.A., 42¼ tons.

For general merchandise, which passes in relatively small quantities and requires a quick daily service, there is practically no demand for wagons of a greater capacity than the standard 12-ton wagon. Road competition and the trend of modern industry have combined to impose upon railways the necessity of providing rapid transit and quick delivery, both of which would be impossible if larger wagons were to be economically utilized. Actually truck loads for merchandise work out at a low average of about 3 tons per wagon, but this is due to the difference between axle load and cubic capacity. The quantity of merchandise which a 12-ton wagon will carry varies from its maximum to as little as 12 cwt. of wickerwork or 24 cwt. of returned empties. To secure rapid transit in the interest of traders, wagons are dispatched if a direct load of even as little as one ton is available. Otherwise delay would result from transhipment, or waiting for full loads.

On the other hand, certain classes of traffic, such as coal, ores, steel bars, road stone, granite, bricks, and crude chemicals, lend themselves with advantage to conveyance in wagons up to 20 tons or more capacity. For example, 50-ton trucks are used to convey bricks from Fletton and sulphate of ammonia from Haverton Hill to Middlesbrough Dock, while 40-ton trucks are employed by the L.M.S.R. to bring coal to one of its electric power stations.[5] The N.E.R. (now incorporated in the L.N.E.R.) has for many years utilized high capacity wagons because in its area the bulk of the coal was exported and the custom had arisen of employing company's wagons for this traffic. Fully 90 per cent. of the coal shipped at ports between Blyth and Middlesbrough is carried in 20-ton wagons. The G.W.R. in 1923 offered a rebate of 5 per cent. of the conveyance charges for coal carried in fully loaded 20-ton wagons, and in 1925 it reduced the charges on the tipping and weighing of these wagons. The results have not been

[5] Before the war the Caledonian Railway owned over four hundred 30-ton bogie merchandise wagons and had experimented with 50-ton wagons. (Protheroe, *Railways of the World*, p. 478.)

very favourable, and in 1930 considerably less than one million tons of coal were shipped from 20-ton wagons at South Wales ports.

Twenty-ton wagons are the exception rather than the rule in this country, and including both private owners' and companies' wagons, they represent only about 3 per cent. of the total number of mineral wagons. Yet 20-ton wagons have undoubted advantages for mineral traffic, and their more general adoption would do much to reduce the costs of handling such traffic besides increasing the efficiency of the railways in other directions. Comparing a 20-ton wagon with a 10-ton wagon, an increase in capacity of 100 per cent. is obtained; but the tare weight is only 33 to 50 per cent. more; the capital cost is only about 50 per cent. greater and the length is from 16 to 30 per cent. more; maintenance charges show a saving of about 25 per cent.; locomotives could haul larger paying loads amounting to about 25 per cent. more, and shunting would be reduced by reason of the fewer wagons required.[6] Experience on the Continent goes to show that there is no greater breakage of coal in the larger wagons.

The difficulties in the way of the adoption of larger wagons in the coal trade lie mainly in the necessity of re-equipping collieries and ports to take the larger wagons. Screens, weigh-bridges, and sidings in the collieries, and hoists, tips, etc., at the ports would have to be altered in certain districts, and this, together with alterations in certain works sidings, has been estimated to involve a cost of about £8,750,000. Another difficulty is the disinclination of the traders to use the larger wagons, and in the retail coal trade the organization is at present such that even the 12-ton wagon is sometimes too large.

In France, Belgium, and Germany, mineral wagons are generally railway owned, and the standard capacity is 20 tons. The conditions are somewhat different in that the use of the wagons is not confined to the coal trade and the

---

[6] See evidence by Mr. W. T. Stephenson, Report of Royal Commission on the Coal Industry, pp. 97-8.

lay-out of sidings in the mining areas is not so cramped.[7] The Standing Committee on Mineral Transport has recommended that 20-ton wagons should be more generally employed for coal and coke traffic subject to the adaptation of terminal facilities at collieries and works.

The economies possible through the use of 20-ton wagons may be illustrated by taking an example of a number of coal shipments totalling 72,000 tons. A locomotive could haul and sidings could accommodate 50 20-ton wagons, giving a gross load of about 1,450 tons, but with 12-ton wagons the trains would probably have to be restricted to 60 wagons, giving a gross load of 1,140 tons. One hundred trains of 12-ton wagons would be required, but only seventy-two trains of 20-ton wagons would be necessary, and the non-paying tare weight would be 1,050 tons less in the latter case. The total net saving which would follow the adoption of 20-ton wagons for all mineral traffic has been estimated at roughly £2,000,000 per annum.

### RAILWAY DOCKS AND HARBOURS

The four railway groups own 78 docks and harbours with a water area of 2,584 acres and representing a capital expenditure of £65,000,000.

Prior to 1914 the charging powers of a railway-owned dock were restricted to certain maxima prescribed in the Act authorizing its construction or in some subsequent Act regulating its charges. Actually the charges levied were slightly below the prescribed maxima. During the war no increase in charges was made until 1918, when an increase of 50 per cent. was permitted by the Board of Trade. In 1920 charges were again raised to amounts 150 per cent. above those of 1914, but later they were reduced to 60 per cent. above pre-war level. Except in Scotland, where the temporary Acts of 1920-22 are still in force, the dock charges of the four groups are now regu-

[7] See report by Mr. C. E. R. Sherrington, Report of the Royal Commission on the Coal Industry. Appendix 23.

lated by Private Acts promoted in 1930 and 1931, but the charges may be periodically reviewed by the Minister of Transport.

The railway ownership of docks has been a subject of considerable controversy and a great deal can be said on both sides of the question. The problem centres mainly on the level of charges imposed by the railways, and the facilities available for exchange of traffic between ocean vessels and road or canal transport. Should the charges be such as to cover the whole costs of the dock, or may the railways take into account the contributory value of the traffic? The question must be considered from the standpoint of broad economic principles before it can be decided whether or not the public will suffer from such discrimination. The case for the railways may be stated as follows. The work of transportation might be divided roughly into two parts: (1) the transit of commodities and (2) the provision of terminal services. Now it may be argued that the work of the port is part and parcel of the whole transportation process just as is that of a goods station. The general principle underlying railway charging is to regard all costs in the aggregate and then to apportion them on the basis of charging 'what the traffic will bear'. If the services of the docks are regarded in this light, then the total costs of providing rail transport and dock services might be aggregated and apportioned as seems best, i.e. so as to secure the best return on the whole. Economic theory shows as the result of a somewhat abstruse application of the mathematical method that the consumer will benefit if two monopolies, each supplying part of a single service (e.g. in the present case a dock and a railway), are in the hands of one monopolist, whereas if each is in the hands of separate monopolists, the consumer will have to pay more. No doubt this theoretical proposition may not apply very exactly to practical conditions of railway and dock charging, but it affords an interesting confirmation of the proposition that the consumer may gain through the combined ownership of docks and railways.

From the railway point of view a dock is regarded as bringing traffic to the railway. Therefore a loss in one direction might mean a gain in another. Better opportunities also are afforded for the control of traffic, and this is of especial importance in coal shipping ports such as those in Northumberland and Durham. Finally it is to be observed that many British ports owe their origin and development to the enterprise of railways in the past.

From the standpoint of the community, however, it is necessary that docks should be also available to road transport and that facilities should be provided for the transfer of cargo from ocean-going vessels to coasting steamers or canal barges. If this were not provided by a railway-owned dock, there would so far be a case for Government intervention, but it is generally agreed that the railways in this country do provide such facilities.

The Royal Commission on Transport stated that they were not at all certain that it would be to the public advantage to transfer railway-owned docks and harbours from their present ownership considering the character of the great majority of such docks and harbours. Many of them, e.g. Fishguard, Folkestone, Harwich, Heysham, and Newhaven, are almost of the nature of stations providing a link between the railways and the steamboats. A very large proportion of the remainder are used almost exclusively for coal shipments. With regard to Southampton, which is one of the two large general ports in railway ownership, the Commission believed that its wonderful development in recent years was largely due to the enterprise of the London and South-Western Railway (now incorporated in the Southern Railway).[8]

[8] *Final Report*, p. 135.

CHAPTER XIV

# ECONOMICS OF RAILWAY ELECTRIFICATION

## THE ECONOMICS OF ELECTRIC TRACTION

THE essential feature of electric traction is the removal of power generation from the train to a stationary power unit, and this fact is responsible for most of its economies and advantages. This same fact also gives rise to the great drawback of electrification, since a large amount of capital has to be expended in providing the overhead or third-rail equipment, together with the necessary feeders, transmission cables, and sub-stations. This capital once expended is definitely tied to the route and cannot be moved if the scheme does not prove a financial success.

The elimination of the boiler and the reciprocating parts of the steam engine give an important advantage to the electric locomotive in regard to repairs and maintenance costs. Moreover, an electric locomotive can be kept more continuously in service than a steam locomotive; probably for about 80 per cent. of the year as compared with 40 per cent. for steam locomotives. The incidence of labour cost in operating is reduced as double-heading requires only one crew and multiple-unit trains can be driven by one motor-man. Labour is not required for lighting fires, raising steam, or for coaling, watering, and cleaning fires, and shed staffs can therefore be reduced. Along with the elimination of movements to turn-tables, these advantages also mean a saving in time at terminal stations.

The electric motor able to draw upon the power resources of large generating stations has a greater overload capacity

176

than the steam engine, and this, together with the greater powers of acceleration also possible, enables it to maintain better average speeds over difficult routes. Uniform speeds among different classes of trains or over different sections of line are possible to a much greater extent where electric traction is employed than is the case with steam. The tracks available can therefore be utilized to better advantage. The steam engine is a constant output machine, so that with heavy loads speed has to be considerably reduced on rising gradients. For example, in the United States until 1912 the ' Fast Denver Limited ', a crack express train, had to negotiate Soldier Summit over the Wasatch Mountains on a grade of 1 in 25, but to maintain the scheduled speed, four header engines and one pusher had to be employed.

On downward gradients the braking of electric trains is more efficient. Indeed, economy in power consumption can be obtained through regenerative braking whereby current is fed back into the electric conductors and used to assist other trains on the upward gradients. Where three-phase motors are employed there are no difficulties in adopting this system.[1] The regenerative braking effect is very efficient, and where heavy goods trains are concerned there is a marked reduction in the wear of brake shoes, wheels, tyres, and rails. Mechanical braking equipment must be provided, however, in case a short circuit puts the electric braking out of action.

The centralization of power supply provided by the generating station enables more efficient steam plant to be employed than is possible in the confined and restricted mechanism of a locomotive. Electric operation has the additional advantage of eliminating the smoke nuisance. Apart from the general gain to the community, which cannot be measured in money values, this increases the comfort of passengers, reduces the cost of carriage and station cleaning, and permits a clear view of signals. These

---

[1] Current may also be regenerated from direct current motors, except that if mercury arc rectifiers are used the energy has to be dissipated in resistances.

M

advantages make electric traction practically essential for underground railways and long tunnelled sections of line.

The extent of railway electrification in various countries where it has made most progress is shown in the following table:

### RAILWAY ELECTRIFICATION IN 1930

|  | Route mileage electrified. | Proportion of total mileage. |
|---|---|---|
| Switzerland . . . | 1,542 | 32 % |
| Austria . . . . | 443 | 11·3 % |
| Italy . . . . | 1,013 | 8·1 % |
| Sweden . . . . | 726 | 7·6 % |
| France . . . . | 1,048 | 3·2 % |
| Great Britain* . . . | 555 | 2·8 % |
| Germany . . . . | 968 | 2·5 % |
| United States . . . | 1,870 | 0·7 % |

* Including 59 miles under construction, but excluding Tube lines.

In Switzerland, Italy, Austria, and parts of France electrification has been due to geographical factors. In these mountainous regions coal supplies are lacking, but there is abundant water power, gradients are severe, and there are numerous tunnels. The conditions therefore favour electric traction, but are less suitable to steam operation. In Italy, for example, regenerative braking on the more steeply graded sections enables as much as 20 to 25 per cent. of the current consumed in ascending to be returned on the downward grades. In the United States, gradients, tunnels, or traffic congestion have been the main reasons for electrification, but experience has shown that a heavy volume of traffic is essential for success. For example, 650 miles of the Milwaukee Railroad were electrified, but the line was forced into bankruptcy because of lack of traffic even though electric operation had reduced working costs.

## SUBURBAN ELECTRIFICATION

In suburban areas, where traffic is dense, electrification has important advantages. The heavy capital cost is spread over a large number of traffic units, and once the equipment has been installed, frequent services can be provided since the cost of running extra trains is small. Headways can be reduced because the trains have great powers of acceleration and rapid braking is possible, and if double-headed train units are used, engine-shunting is avoided at terminals. The cost of stopping an electric train is also less; roughly a stop costs about 6d. to 1s. as compared with 1s. 6d. to 3s. for a similar steam train. Another advantage is the more rapid crossing of fouling points. One motorman only is required, and the labour costs per train are reduced. The elimination of coaling, watering, and turn-table movements also increases the capacity of terminal stations, while the elimination of smoke is important at large and busy stations and enhances the value of adjoining property. With the multiple-unit system of trains, the number of coaches can be adjusted to the traffic, and operating costs are decreased proportionally, whereas there would be little economy in varying the composition of steam-train links. Where traffic has outgrown track capacity, electrification enables more trains to be operated on existing tracks, thus obviating the necessity of expensive track duplications.

In Great Britain, except for the L.N.E.R. Newport to Shildon line (18 miles), electrification has been confined to passenger services in suburban areas. In all, 496 route miles, exclusive of Tube Railways, have been electrified up to the present time of writing, and a further 59 miles are under construction. Of the completed mileage 105 miles belong to the L.M.S.R., 32 miles to the L.N.E.R., and 56 miles to the Metropolitan and District Railway. The Southern Railway has made most progress in electrification, and its 276 route miles (equivalent to 750 track miles) gives it the distinction of possessing the largest suburban electric railway system in the world. The first stage in this company's programme of electrification has now been completed, but an additional 51 miles is in hand on the route from Purley to Brighton and Worthing. This is almost a main-line scheme, but it has been undertaken for suburban traffic reasons as there is a large daily movement of passengers between London and the coast.

The electrification of suburban routes on the Southern Railway has proved very successful, and at the Annual Meeting of that company in 1930 the Chairman was able to state that ' the increase in traffic in the electrified area is progressing at a pace which has considerably exceeded all expectations '. The electric services can provide 7·8 million train-miles per annum as compared with the 4·4 million which was possible with steam traction. In 1930 the number of passengers increased on the Southern Railway, though on all the other grouped railways there was a decrease. This was due to an increase of over 12,500,000 in the number of suburban passengers in the electrified area. The number of season-ticket holders has grown from 166,800 in 1925 to 189,468 in 1930. No doubt part of the increase is due to the recent economic development of the southern parts of the Kingdom and to the greater industrial prosperity of the London area as compared with other parts. However this may be, electrification has provided the means of carrying the increased traffic and has placed the company in a stronger position to compete with road transport.

The electric trains on the Southern Railway are operated on the 600 volt direct-current third-rail system, which obviates unsightly and complicated overhead equipment and gives a better view to the drivers. Permanent-way men, however, have to be equipped with insulated tools, and marshalling yards and freight depôts are worked by steam, since the third-rail system would be too dangerous.

In 1927 the Pringle Committee recommended the adoption of a 1,500 volt overhead-conductor system for future schemes of electrification, and this has been adopted as the basis of the Weir Report. The first passenger line in this country to be worked on this system was the Manchester, South Junction, and Altrincham Railway, which was electrified in 1931. This line is jointly owned by the L.M.S.R. and the L.N.E.R. and is nine miles in length, serving a densely populated district.

### MAIN LINE ELECTRIFICATION

In this country main line electrification has made no progress up to the present, and it has generally been held that the large capital expenditure necessary would not be justified except in those few places where a dense traffic was available. A clear distinction has been drawn between suburban and main line electrification. The one has been regarded as desirable and economic, but the other has been considered impossible of realization. Nor can it be urged that the success of main line electrification in other countries is any argument for electrification in this country, because conditions are entirely different.[2] If a case is to be made out for electrification of the main lines in Great Britain, new arguments have to be adduced, and the problem considered solely in the light of the conditions prevailing in this country. The main factor is the amount of traffic on a line, because the extra cost involved is very largely a fixed sum per mile of track, while the saving effected in running costs is a definite sum per train mile.

[2] Actually continental electric systems have not proved very remunerative despite their use of cheap electric power generated by falling water. The Swiss Federal Railway in 1929 showed a net surplus of only £200,000 in the working of their electric lines after allowing for interest charges and amortization of capital. Yet in Switzerland the economic conditions are exceptionally favourable. In Sweden, the full advantages of electric traction have only been obtained by fitting all trains with continuous brakes. In Germany electrification has been due in part to a desire to use water power and in part to the pressure of the powerful electrical industries. In France the electrified railways have not shown a profit, though it is impossible to say how far this has been due to electrification or not.

THE WEIR COMMITTEE REPORT

In 1929 a committee consisting of Lord Weir (Chairman), Sir Ralph Wedgwood, and Sir William McLintock was appointed by the Minister of Transport to report on the economic and other aspects of railway electrification in Great Britain, with particular reference to main line working. Their report was issued in 1931 and they did not put forward definite recommendations, as they were not required to do so.[3]   In this important report the essential points brought out are: (a) that the recent establishment of the national electric ' grid ' has greatly increased the prospects for electrification; (b) that dual working by steam and electricity is uneconomical and expensive and that a complete scheme of electrification is necessary for success, and (c) that better and more frequent services could be economically provided by electric working than by steam operation. The report anticipated that a surplus of about 2 per cent. would be available as a result of electrification after allowing for interest charges on the new capital required. This assumes that the traffic of 1929 would be maintained, but having regard to the heavy fixed charges involved, it is pointed out in the report, any increase in traffic as a result of electrification or revived trade would increase the savings over steam. This may well be the case, but on the other hand any considerable falling off in traffic would turn the small estimated profit into a serious loss. Since 1929 there has been a decline of traffic, and the small return on capital allows no margin for a reduction of rates and fares which might be necessary to attract lost traffic back to the railways.

The Committee, in order to obtain reliable comparisons of the costs of steam and electric traction, arranged for detailed estimates to be prepared for two sections of main line, one comprising practically all the old G.N.R. section

[3] Report of the Committee on Main Line Electrification, 55-164 (1931.)

of the L.N E.R. and the other the L.M.S.R. main line from Crewe to Liverpool and Carlisle. In the former it was assumed that the whole of the surrounding lines would be electrified, but in the second that the surrounding lines would be operated by steam, thus involving a certain amount of dual working. The results of these investigations are shown in the following table.

| ESTIMATES FOR ELECTRIFICATION OF CERTAIN SECTIONS OF MAIN LINE | | |
|---|---|---|
| | L.N.E.R. | L.M.S.R. |
| Total route mileage involved . | 492 | 193 |
| Total track mileage involved . | 1,944 | 843 |
| Trailing ton-miles per annum. Electric . . . . | 6,000,000,000 | 2,225,000,000 |
| Trailing ton-miles per annum. Steam . . . . | —— | 395,000,000 |
| Engine-miles. Electric . | 21,000,000 | 7,950,000 |
| Engine-miles. Steam . . | —— | 1,590,000 |
| Traffic density (trailing ton-miles per running track mile per annum) . . . (Average for whole country 3,000,000) | 4,300,000 | 4,050,000 |
| Net capital outlay . . | £8,646,000 | £5,123,000 |
| Savings in working expenses . | £624,600 | £127,800 |
| Percentage return on capital . | 7·22% | 2·5% |

The low return of 2·5 per cent. on capital expenditure on the L.M.S.R. section as compared with the L.N.E.R. section (7·22 per cent.) is due to the small extent of the former and the amount of dual working involved. The Committee therefore concluded that the full benefits of electrification would only be obtained by the complete adoption of electric traction. Experience on the Swiss Federal, the Paris-Orleans, the Swedish State, and the Southern Railways all point to the same conclusion. Moreover it is only on the basis of complete electrification that the low price of ·475d. per unit for electric energy is possible as estimated in the Report, and then only if the estimates for the extension of the National Grid proved accurate.[4]

The Committee also obtained estimates for the cost of complete electrification of the whole railway system, but these, unlike the estimates described above, were based on broad assumptions and were not the result of detailed investigations and actual surveys. The Report states, however, that they were compiled on a conservative basis. In the following two tables the estimated capital cost of complete electrification and comparative working costs for steam and electric traction as given in the Report are summarized.

### TABLE I

ESTIMATED CAPITAL COST OF ELECTRIFICATION OF ALL STANDARD
GAUGE RAILWAYS IN GREAT BRITAIN

|  |  | £ millions |
|---|---|---|
| (1) | Track equipment . . . . | 129·7 |
| (2) | Auxiliary power cable . . . | 13·5 |
| (3) | Alterations to ways and works . . | 13·7 |
| (4) | Electric tractors . . . . | 136·5 |
| (5) | Running sheds, shops, stores, etc. . | 4·5 |
| (6) | Spare parts . . . . . | 5·5 |
| (7) | Auxiliary power supplies . . . | 2·25 |
| (8) | Interest during construction . . | 12·5 |
| (9) | Engineering expenses . . . | 5·0 |

Total gross cost  323·15

CREDIT ITEMS
(FROM SALE OF STOCK OR OTHERWISE)

|  |  | £ millions |  |
|---|---|---|---|
| (10) | Steam tractors . . . | 45·5 |  |
| (11) | Coal stocks . . . . | 1·38 |  |
| (12) | Spare parts . . . . | 4·5 |  |
| (13) | Locomotive coal wagons . . | 2·4 |  |
| (14) | Passenger coaches . . . | 2·5 |  |
| (15) | Surplus plant, etc. . . . | 4·0 |  |
| (16) | Train lighting sets . . . | 2·0 |  |

Total credits  62·28   62·28

Net capital cost  £260·87

[4] In certain quarters, railway electrification is being urged in order to provide an increased load for the grid, which at present is working below capacity, but in considering the case for electric traction as an economic proposition, such arguments introduce wider issues than can be dealt with here.

(17) Additional expenditure on generating plant transmission lines and substations, to be incurred by the Central Electricity Board. Interest on this to be included in the price paid for electric energy by the railways . £80,000,000

## TABLE II

ESTIMATE OF COMPARATIVE WORKING COSTS, STEAM AND ELECTRIC
*(including only items affected by electrification)*

|  | £<br>Steam | £<br>Electric | £<br>Saving |
|---|---|---|---|
| (1) Locomotive fuel or electric energy . | 12,310,446 | 11,280,000 | 1,030,446 |
| (2) Locomotive wages . | 20,933,425 | 10,778,712 | 10,154,713 |
| (3) Repairs of tractors . | 10,819,012 | 4,660,000 | 6,159,012 |
| (4) Water for locomotives | 883,666 | — | 883,666 |
| (5) Stores, clothing, and miscellaneous . | 905,992 | 453,000 | 452,992 |
| (6) Lubrication . . | 290,415 | 102,000 | 188,415 |
| (7) Maintenance of engine sheds and shops | 436,959 | 175,000 | 261,959 |
| (8) Guards' wages . | 4,296,462 | 3,653,462 | 643,000 |
| (9) Cleansing of vehicles | 933,500 | 700,000 | 233,400 |
| (10) Insurance, pensions, etc. | 794,250 | 397,150 | 397,100 |
| (11) Saving on maintenance of train lighting sets | — | — | 513,000 |
| (12) Savings on auxiliary power and light supplies . . | — | — | 840,000 |

Total saving £21,757,703

ADDITIONAL COSTS OF ELECTRIFICATION
(13) Maintenance and renewals of electric track equipment . . . 3,385,000
(14) Maintenance and operation of sub-stations . . . . 1,056,000
(15) Increase in depreciation (renewals) of electric tractors compared with steam . . . . 20,000

Total £4,461,000

Gross savings due to electrification . . £21,757,703
Deduct extra costs of electrification . . 4,461,000

Net saving due to electrification . . . 17,296,703
Additional net revenue on haulage of coal to power stations . . . . 254,000

£17,550,703

equivalent to 6·7% on £261,000,000

On the basis of these estimates, both general and detailed, the Committee anticipated that there would be a surplus of approximately 2 per cent. available after meeting interest charges on the new capital, assuming that existing traffics (1929) were maintained and that the programme took twenty years to complete.

An additional capital expenditure of £45,000,000 would be necessary for suburban electrification, but this the Committee considered would be the most remunerative portion of a general electrification scheme. A saving of £5·85 millions was estimated, equivalent to a return of 13 per cent. on the extra capital. The Report did not favour the suggestion that the first step should be the electrification of suburban areas. They admitted that 'the suggestion is attractive at first sight, but in our opinion it should be treated with caution, as it seems probable that in many cases the handicap of dual working, to which we have already drawn attention, might subsequently affect the financial return due to increased suburban traffic'. On the other hand, the Report points out that certain branch lines might continue to be worked by independent power units, such as oil-electric or steam locomotives where traffic is light, but in framing the estimates it was found impossible to separate such sections. Some savings would accrue if this policy were followed.

The most obvious criticism of the Report is the very large capital expenditure involved and the smallness of the estimated return. This is admitted in the Report, but it is urged that other factors must be taken into account which are not capable of a direct monetary assessment, e.g. future economic development of the country or increase of traffic as a result of improved services. Soon after the Report was issued, however, financial stringency and the need for national economy became the foremost problems of the day and any possibility of State aid was ruled out of the question, though indirectly it was hinted at by a reference to the amount of money spent by the Government on the roads.

The importance of the contribution of the Weir Committee Report lies in the fact that for the first time since a national supply of electricity became available a definite estimate has been given of the costs of general railway electrification and calculations have been presented for detailed criticism. The Committee itself admitted that there are certain risks and contingencies involved in arriving at conclusions based on the estimates. ' Put shortly, the risks involved in undertaking a comprehensive programme cannot be predicted with accuracy. They lie in the fallibility of estimates, in the possibilities of reduction in traffic due to further development of road transport, or to reduced national activity, and finally in the field of speculative scientific development.' The margin of error cannot be determined until, as was suggested in the Report, a considerable portion of some main line is surveyed in detail.

## CRITICISM OF THE REPORT

In the first place, certain estimates, such as the credits allowed for the sale of part-worn steam locomotives or the value assigned to steam parts which could be used up without replacement, must be of necessity very speculative, and probably the estimates would be found to be on the generous side. Then during the period of twenty years required to complete the programme of electrification, certain locomotives used on specific routes might require renewal but might not be available from redundant stock of other sections. Also during the conversion period there would be a considerable disorganization in traffic arrangements and dual working might be necessary, but no allowance seems to have been made for this.

The estimates also allow for only one driver on multiple-unit trains, goods trains, and shunting engines, though for long-distance passenger trains a driver and an assistant are allowed. This might meet with opposition, despite the fact that on suburban routes the present custom is to have one motorman only.

No detailed economic investigations were made into the probable price trends of coal, but much depends on this factor. If the price of electricity were reduced to the low figure of ·475d. per unit suggested in the Report, there would be a reduction in fuel costs of somewhat under 9 per cent., but the calculation would be upset by any variation in relative costs.

The Report reverses previous ideas of the advantages and limitations of electric traction which were based on considerations of the heavy capital costs involved. This the Committee were able to do by charging a proportion of the overhead charges normally borne by an electric railway to the Central Electricity Board, which declared that it could supply current at a cost much less than the railways could have produced it themselves. No doubt large scale production would be much cheaper and a greater equalization of load could be obtained on the grid system, but this aspect of the problem requires further investigation.

The average cost of electrification per mile on which the capital costs are based in the Report, works out at a figure considerably less than that which was necessary in the case of the Southern Railway Company's electrification programme, though the somewhat cheaper third rail system was used. Also the costs set against electric locomotives would appear to be low, while it is not certain that such intensive use could be made of them as is suggested because the average might be reduced by traffic requirements. Workshops would also require to be converted from steam to electric locomotive construction and repair, and this might involve some further expenditure.

Other matters requiring the most careful consideration are the possible development of road transport in the near future and the possible improvement of the steam engine. The Committee also does not appear to have given suffi-cient attention to the possibilities of the oil-electric loco-motive, which has shown signs of great development in the near future. Once the railways committed themselves to extensive main line electrification, it would be impossible to change over to other forms of traction owing to the financial sacrifice which would be involved.

### THE CASE FOR THE STEAM LOCOMOTIVE

An account of the problems of railway electrification would be incomplete without some reference to the advan-tages of the steam locomotive. The steam engine is a self-contained power unit and is not dependent on the provision of elaborate and expensive electric equipment. Therefore a failure in power supply does not stop the working of the whole system, and the capital cost of the line is much less than with electric traction. As compared with the petrol or diesel engine, it is cheaper in first cost, its construction is much simpler, it is a more flexible power unit, and its parts do not have to work at such high speeds. Improvements are still being effected in the steam engine, among which may be mentioned the use of very high steam pressures, a development which is still in its infancy.

A common delusion is that higher speeds are possible with electric traction than with steam locomotives, but the truth is that the limiting factors to speed—internal mechani-cal friction, wind resistance, curves, etc.—apply equally to both forms of traction. The fastest trains in the world are hauled by steam locomotives, and if speed alone were the consideration, the steam engine would provide it at less capital cost than electric locomotives. Electric traction has only advantages in regard to speed on gradients and in acceleration. Even as regards acceleration, the steam loco-motive, if suitably designed, can make out a good case for itself, and in the United States average speeds of 60 m.p.h. start to stop are worked by steam trains over short distances of from 10 to 30 miles.

To conclude this brief description of the advantages of the steam engine there may well be quoted the cogent and practical remarks of an experienced engine-driver, Mr. Ben Glasgow, who worked for forty-three years on the foot-plate, and drove the first non-stop train from London to Edinburgh.

If the electricians think that they can beat the ' Pacific ' engines they have got something to do—I mean for speed and power and reliability and economy.  Five hundred and eight tons you can have behind you and get in to time, on thirty-eight or forty pounds of coal to the mile.  And remember the engine is running the auxiliary plant as well for fourteen cars, with all the dynamos for lighting, cooking, and fans, and steam for heating.[5]

### THE OIL-ELECTRIC AND OTHER TYPES OF LOCOMOTIVES

Great strides have recently been taken in the improvement of the diesel engine, and already promising results have been achieved with this form of locomotive in various countries.  The thermal efficiency of the oil engine is high compared with the ordinary non-condensing type of steam locomotive, but for technical reasons it is not possible to adopt a direct drive.  Therefore the oil engine is used to drive an electric generator, which in turn supplies current to an electric motor geared to the wheels.

The cost of operating is higher than that of electric traction in the case of very dense traffic, but it is claimed that on all other services the oil-electric engine would give all the advantages of electrification—viz. rapid acceleration, high average speed, absence of smoke, reduction in labour cost, and increased availability since less time is required for overhauls and maintenance duties than is necessary with steam engines—but would not necessitate the stereotyping of traction methods as would electric operation. Further advantages are that fuel is not consumed while an oil-electric locomotive is waiting in sidings or at stations, and re-fueling is a very simple matter.  Oil-electric traction could be adopted gradually and the problem of duel working would not arise.  It is claimed that the capital cost required to change over to this system would be only about half that of electrification, but the return would be at least twice as great.

[5] Quoted in the *Railway Gazette*, June 5, 1931, pp. 821-2.

As compared with the steam locomotive, the main disadvantages of the oil-electric locomotive are its greater capital cost, its weight, and the fact that a home-produced fuel cannot be used. If, however, oil could be obtained from coal on a commercial scale, the situation would be considerably changed in favour of the oil-electric locomotive. At present the oil-electric locomotive is only in its experimental stage, but it would appear that rapid progress will be made in the near future by this type of locomotive.

The remaining alternatives to electrification which have been suggested are an increased use of light steam rail cars for improving frequency of service, and more speculatively the development of the storage battery locomotive. In the Irish Free State the Drumm Battery has been applied to rail traction with results sufficiently satisfactory to encourage further trials. This battery can be charged very quickly, but is said to be heavy and somewhat expensive. Time alone will show if any development will take place in the evolution of this form of locomotive.

## CHAPTER XV

# THE RAILWAYS AND THEIR ROAD TRANSPORT
# SERVICES

THE rapid growth of road transport since the war has had severe reactions on the prosperity of the railways, and this has been the more serious as it has coincided with a period of trade depression. Road competition has been keenest in connexion with short distance traffic and the carriage of commodities in the higher grades of the railway classification, though it has by no means been confined to short journeys and valuable articles. The railway companies have complained that they are not allowed to compete with their rivals on an equal footing in as much as they are restricted by numerous Government regulations and legal disabilities, including the law of undue preference. They are also responsible for the entire capital cost and upkeep of their permanent way, stations, and signalling, whereas they argue that road transport is provided with part of the equivalent equipment at the expense of the community. The total all-in cost of roads and bridges per annum, including police duties, has been estimated at £61,000,000, and the total revenue raised from motor vehicle duties and the petrol tax of 8d. per gallon amount (1932) to about £50,000,000, leaving a balance of about £11,000,000 to be found from other sources.[1]

In competition with the railways, road transport has the economic advantages of flexibility and mobility, which enable door-to-door services to be provided; it is more amenable to the control of the consignor and can be oper-

[1] On the whole question see the author's *Economics of Road Transport* and *Transport Co-ordination*.

ated economically with small loads, and frequent services can be provided even with a comparatively light flow of traffic; handling is also reduced, and delicate articles are less likely to be damaged; responsibility can be definitely allocated, and pilferage risks are therefore less. The elimination of troublesome claims for damage or loss is regarded by traders as a matter of considerable importance. For short distance passenger travel the motor has important advantages in its convenience, frequency of service, cheapness, and flexibility.

Though road and rail transport are competitive, they are also to a large extent complementary, and if the two are used in conjunction they can be used to supplement each other.[2]

Probably the most important development in the transport situation during the past few years has been the growing tendency to recognize this inter-relation between road and rail transport. Though there is still a great deal of rivalry and competition between the two, they are no longer regarded as if they were in completely water-tight compartments. This change has been largely brought about by the passing of the Railway (Road Transport) Acts 1928, which empowered the four grouped railways to invest in road transport concerns and to operate road services on an extended scale. These Acts gave the railways the opportunity to co-ordinate their rail services with road transport, and already considerable use has been made of the new powers. The railwayman now has to develop the 'road-rail outlook' so that every opportunity will be seized for obtaining the greatest advantage from the two powerful instruments of transport placed in his hands.

### CO-ORDINATED PASSENGER SERVICES

As a result of numerous agreements and mergers effected by the railway companies with important motor-bus firms, there is now a very large measure of co-ordination as regards road and rail passenger transport. The railway

[2] See the author's *Transport Co-ordination*, Chapter V.

N

companies, on obtaining their road transport powers, did not attempt to start road passenger services of their own but were content to obtain a financial interest in established motor-bus concerns, generally to the extent of 50 per cent. of the capital. Now practically every motor-bus company and several municipalities are combined in this way with the railway companies in providing transport services. Co-ordinating Committees, consisting of representatives of the road and rail interests in equal numbers, have been set up in various areas for the joint consideration of methods of co-ordination. The committees have already accomplished excellent work, and they are continuing to explore the possibilities of further co-operation in their localities. One of the first steps taken was to make some alterations in time-tables so that passengers could make connexions between the two services. This was followed by the sub-stitution of bus services for branch line passenger trains in districts where the branch lines were unremunerative. The bus concerns have diverted their services in certain towns so as to include the railway station as one of their stopping places, or the station yard has been used as a parking place for the buses. The proposed new G.W.R. station at Cardiff is to be a great combined railway and motor-bus station.

A great deal of progress has been made as regards through bookings by road and rail and in extending the inter-availability of tickets, though the latter involves many difficult problems. In the spring of 1931 inter-availability was in operation between 842 places, and this included not only ordinary tickets but also in certain areas excur-sion, cheap day and period tickets, and even 'seasons'. Inter-availability has also been extended to long distance motor-coach tickets. Thus the G.W.R. has arranged for such facilities between London and Penzance, Barnstaple, St. Ives, Falmouth, and Ifracombe, among other places. Passengers are allowed to send their luggage in advance on the usual terms, and in this way one of the difficulties inseparable from co-ordinated road and rail services has been overcome. Inter-availability has also been arranged by the L.N.E.R. in respect of journeys between London and Clacton-on-Sea, Dovercourt Bay and Harwich, on payment of a reasonable supplementary fare when rail is used. It is general to charge a supplementary fare of this nature, equivalent to the difference in the single fare between road and rail tickets. Certain difficulties are naturally involved in arranging for the exchange of tickets, especially as both the railways and the motor-bus companies have developed their own systems of issuing and controlling tickets. Each system has worked well in its own sphere, but they are not easily combined. Extension of inter-available ticket arrangements should enable the railway companies to take off trains after the busy hours on certain branch lines. In many cases late trains are exceedingly expensive to run.

Co-ordinated parcel services have recently been introduced by the G.W.R. and the S.R. in conjunction with their associated road companies, and possibly in the future these facilities will be considerably extended. The G.W.R. scheme permits of parcels up to one hundredweight in weight being booked through from London or any G.W.R. station to some forty towns or villages in outlying districts within twenty miles of Oxford, and in each of these towns or villages agents have been appointed to receive and hand over the parcels.

The correlation of road and rail passenger services has thus made considerable progress, and the facilities offer a greatly improved transport service to the public which would be impossible if each were operated independently of the other.

Recently the L.M.S.R. has introduced a vehicle known as a 'Ro-railer' which can travel either on the road or on rails. The change-over can be effected in less than five minutes as no special equipment is required other than the levelling up of the ground for a few yards to rail level. It has been suggested that there is scope for such vehicles or truck-trailers constructed on similar principles for operation on branch lines or in sparsely populated districts. Time alone, however, will show whether or not the combined vehicle can be utilized with advantage.

## GOODS SERVICES

There has been considerable development in the provision of road haulage services by the railways since they obtained their extended road powers in 1928. In contrast with the policy of combination with established road concerns on the passenger side, the railways have adopted a policy of providing road goods services of their own. Partly this difference has been due to the less highly organized character of the road haulage industry and partly to the desire of the railway companies to retain control of the co-ordinated lorries so that they might be used as an instrument for the development of rail traffic.

## CARTAGE SERVICES

The collection and delivery of traffic by road has long been an important feature of British railway practice. In foreign countries these services have been left to other concerns, though now there is a marked tendency to adopt the British policy. The cartage services of pre-war days, however, were limited in area to a radius of a few miles around the stations and depôts, but since 1918 the services have been extended, and it is now lawful for the railways to undertake direct road haulage without an intermediate rail haul.

The problems involved in the organization and operation of cartage services are problems of road transport economics rather than railway economics.[3] In the first place it is essential that accurate costs should be kept week by week so that waste and excessive expenditure can be checked. This is especially important as the nature of the work tends to raise costs to a high figure owing to the amount of empty

[3] See the author's *Economics of Road Transport*.

or light mileage which has to be worked.   Therefore, in the second place special attention must be directed to obtaining the best use from the vehicles.   Organization must be developed with the object of cutting down terminal delays and empty mileage to the minimum.   Unfortunately full control is not in the company's hands, since traders may be responsible for considerable delays at their works and warehouses.

At the larger goods depôts there are possibilities in the provision of mechanical handling appliances, though generally the miscellaneous character of the loads reduces the economies possible by the use of labour-saving devices. Demountable bodies can sometimes be provided for motor vehicles, or several rulleys can be used for each horse if there is any considerable delay experienced in loading or unloading.

Special attention must be paid to the choice of vehicle, whether horse, petrol motor, electric battery vehicle, or ' steamer '.   Each of these has advantages over the others in certain circumstances or for certain types of traffic, though if traffic is very varied, there may be disadvantages in adopting a mixed fleet.   The decision as to choice in each case must depend on a close study of the characteristics of the traffic and of the operating costs of each type.   A broad division can be drawn between the sphere for horse transport and motor haulage.   Petrol lorries are best suited for the longer delivery rounds, where the stops are spaced out over fair distances.   Horse vehicles can be operated more cheaply where distances are short, or where frequent stopping and starting is involved. They have advantages also where there is considerable traffic congestion on the roads and where warehouse entries are inconveniently situated.   In such circumstances the greater speed of the motor-vehicle cannot be exploited and the low ton-mileage operated makes costs heavier than with the less expensive horse vehicle.   For these reasons railway cartage services have favoured horse haulage in the past.   There is now, however, a tendency to adopt motor vehicles on a larger scale owing to the extension of the services over longer distances, but for local cartage work the horse vehicle still remains the more economical. Experiments have recently been carried out with light tractor units capable of drawing the ordinary horse rulleys, and these have given promise of providing a successful and more economical substitute for horse traction. The Karrier-L.M.S. tractor, or ' mechanical horse ', has been developed to meet the special needs of railway cartage services, and it can be used so as to involve no alteration or adaptation of vehicles previously drawn by horses. This is effected by an ingenious arrangement whereby the front of the rulley is supported by the rear of the tractor. The ' mechanical horse ' combines the advantages of a motor vehicle with those of horse haulage. It is very easily manœuvred; there is no delay waiting for loading and unloading, as the tractor can quickly be transferred to another vehicle; it is more rapid in its movements than the horse and there is no need to ' scrap ' the old vehicles when mechanical traction is adopted. The L.N.E.R. has also experimented successfully with van tractors of the ' Karrier-Cob ' design and they have proved so successful that thirty-two have been ordered for use at the new goods station at Ashburys, Manchester, where the cartage system will eventually be completely mechanized.

The extension of cartage areas so as to provide extensive collection and delivery services has made very rapid progress since about 1927 or 1928. The G.W.R. has developed its road freight organization so extensively that there is scarcely a village in its territory which is not reached by these services. The L.N.E.R. has been a pioneer in the development of rural lorry services radiating from appropriate base stations to outlying villages and farms, and the L.M.S.R. has also opened distribution centres at a large number of stations. Agricultural requirements, such as artificial manures, linseed cake, etc., are delivered as required to the farm-houses by lorries, which also pick up farm produce for conveying to the station.

By arrangement with the Post Office it has been found possible to extend the ' Cash on Delivery ' facilities to railway consignments.

Road vehicles are also hired out on special contracts covering fixed periods ranging from a day to a year, and arrangements are also made for special deliveries of building materials, pipes, electric cables, etc., direct to the site. Such developments require some adaptation of the railway organization, and it is necessary that local officials should be given powers to quote special rates without delay, based on local road transport costing systems which are an essential requirement.

The railways are now prepared to undertake the haulage of practically every description of commodity by road as well as by rail. Petrol lorries are provided for general merchandise; tipping vehicles for building materials or roadstone; double-deck lorries for livestock, or the collection and return of milk churns; road horse-boxes; and specially designed vehicles for bulky consignments, machinery. iron girders, timber, and boilers. So complete is the range of road transport vehicles available that recently the Southern Railway was able to move the equipment, live-stock, household effects, and the personnel of three farms—lock, stock, and barrel—by means of road and rail to places fifty miles away.

### COMBINED AIR AND RAIL TRANSPORT

In 1931 co-ordination was extended to air transport by the four group railways and the Metropolitan Railway in connexion with the services of Imperial Airways Ltd. This scheme provided for the acceptance of urgent consignments at about 200 stations in Britain for conveyance by express train to London and thence by air freighter to any air port served by Imperial Airways on the Continent or on the route to India. Goods are also accepted in the reverse direction, and arrangements are available for re-forwarding by post or rail from the air termini overseas.

Inclusive charges are made for the services which will be found set out in a handbook entitled *Combined Rates for the Conveyance of Freight by Rail and Air*, published by Imperial Airways Ltd. An additional facility provided is that of ' Cash on Delivery '.

## CONTAINERS

The container is in effect a demountable body which can be slung on either road vehicles or railway trucks. It provides a means whereby goods can be conveyed from door to door without disturbance or re-packing. The great advantage of the container from the point of view of railway operating is that handling costs are reduced. Moreover it encourages larger direct loads and thus helps to solve the problem of the minimum direct wagon load. To the trader the advantages are obvious. There is the direct door-to-door service, packing costs are much reduced, and the cost of returned empties is eliminated. At the same time the risk of damage or pilferage is reduced to the minimum, and containers loaded with valuable commodities, such as artificial silk goods, cigarettes, etc., can be locked and sealed. The container system gives to rail transport that mobility which is such an important feature of road transport while at the same time it retains the advantages of high speed and low rates for bulk traffic which are characteristic of the railways. Not only can containers be delivered within the precincts of works, warehouses, and farms, but electric cables, drain-pipes, dressed stone, or bricks loaded in containers can be sent direct to building sites, fields, or other places where works are in progress. Indeed, a container loaded with building material has been delivered direct from the quarry to the third storey of a partially constructed building. Containers can also be shipped direct from this country to the Continent, and services are already operating to and from France, Germany, Holland, Belgium, and Switzerland. Considering the advantages of the container it is not surprising that they have become very popular. In 1928 the railways had only 350 containers in service, in 1929 the number had risen to over 2,000, and in 1930 to 4,355. In the U.S.A. containers have been employed for a number of years, and they have now been adopted by the French and German railways.

Among the traffics for which the container has already become popular are furniture, window-frames, confectionery, flowers, biscuits, electrical machinery, earthenware, meat, bricks, and radiators. Traffic regarded as particularly susceptible to damage in the ordinary course is very suitable to container conveyance, as the risk of damage is greatly reduced. For example, it was stated recently that out of a consignment of 8,400 porcelain pudding-bowls delivered in one container to the store of a well-known firm, none were broken and only ten were cracked. Various types are provided to meet different requirements, and these include insulated containers suitable for meat and perishable traffic, ' hopper ' types for direct delivery of roadstone, etc., open types for conveyance of bricks, tiles, plants, shrubs, or machinery, and box types for general merchandise. The capacities range from two and a half to four tons, but provided a minimum charge as for one ton per container is paid, the loads need not reach the maximum capacity. A differential rate over and above the rail rate applicable to the consignment is charged, and these differentials range from 5 to 20 per cent. of the ordinary rates. The actual percentage charged depends on the commodity, and these are to be found in a Railway Clearing House publication entitled *Traffic in Railway Containers. Differential Method of Charging*, e.g. bricks 5 per cent. differential, cocoa 10 per cent., incubators 15 per cent., and furniture removals 20 per cent. It has been suggested that a flat rate system of charging should be adopted in order to encourage the use of containers. This has certain attractions, e.g. simplicity and reduction of clerical labour, but the flat rate would have to be an average, and thus might prove too high for articles such as bricks or road metal.[4] In the United States the New York Central and other eastern railroads have adopted a flat rate, applicable to all commodities carried in containers, and the new system is said to have proved attractive to traders and to afford considerable savings in clerical labour.

*Limitation to the Use of Containers.* The return and distribution of containers involves a good deal of empty haulage and is the main source of extra expense in connexion with them. In the future, when the numbers are increased, this might be minimized by the adoption of some form of ' common user ' between the different companies. Another limitation is the lack of adequate crane power to handle containers at certain stations, and before such traffic can be accepted it is necessary to refer to the *Handbook of Railway Stations, etc.* which provides information as to crane power available at all stations, goods depôts, and sidings. Some difficulties have also been experienced in providing suitable low-sided wagons. particularly for traffic requiring the use of vehicles fitted with continuous brakes. Carriage trucks are often employed for the purpose where these are available, and one railway company has recently built special chassis carriages, fitted with fixed chocks and securing chains. In America experiments are being carried out between Cleveland and Toledo, Ohio, with containers mounted on wheels —called ' rail-highway wagons '—which can be transferred directly by means of a ramp to flat rail trucks. It is said that three containers of this type fit on one rail wagon and give 50 per cent. greater carrying capacity than that of the average box car.

### RAILHEAD DELIVERIES

The railhead delivery system combines rapid transit by rail in bulk loads, warehousing of goods, and retail distribution by road. Goods can be sent in full truck loads

---

[4] Compare in this connexion the L.N.E.R. experimental charges based on weight per wagon, which were described in Chapter X.

by express freight trains from factories or ports to be warehoused at the railhead for a short or long period, according to circumstances, and delivered to local clients by the railway company's lorries according to the trader's instructions. In addition, arrangements can be made at certain depôts for services such as controlling stocks, accepting and executing delivery orders, collecting empties, etc. Distributors are thus provided with a rail base upon which dispatches for a particular area can be concentrated and from which a radial road service effects deliveries over a wide area. Deliveries can be given without delay not only to towns and villages, but to farms, barns, or sites where the materials are required. If necessary, supplies can be obtained by retail shops in a few hours by telephoning to the railhead depôt. Railhead services are especially useful to manufacturers and distributors of commodities such as groceries, confectionery, soap, tea, or tobacco, which are retailed by shopkeepers who do not carry heavy stocks. Where a firm has sufficient traffic, vans can be allocated to their work and the firm's name or advertisements can be displayed on the vehicles. Formerly such goods were sent direct to the individual tradesmen, and the consignments were generally chargeable at the ' small parcels scale ', except in so far as a saving could be effected by lumping several orders for one town together and distributing by ' split deliveries '.

Railhead deliveries afford an excellent example of adequate road-rail co-ordination as the system combines the advantages of high speed bulk rail traffic with the door-to-door deliveries and small-scale distribution which are the main assets of road transport.

The trader using railhead deliveries obtains the following advantages:

(1) Low rail rates for bulk consignments, including any exceptional rates applicable.

(2) Express rail transit and rapid delivery.

(3) Reduced packing costs, handling and cartage costs. The goods can be packed in full wagons in the form they

will be delivered to the retailers, whereas if they were sent direct each would have to be specially boxed, or crated. Savings are also obtained from the elimination of returned empties.

(4) Demands can be met immediately from local stocks.

(5) Reduced breakages owing to the provision of ' through ' wagons. Traders may load and unload the wagons themselves, and the wagons may be sealed.

The railway companies have found the railhead system a valuable method of competing with road transport and in building up new business. Operating costs are reduced by the substitution of bulk traffic in full wagon loads for a number of miscellaneous ' smalls ' traffic.

The co-ordination of road and rail transport by means of extended collection and delivery services, containers, and railheads has been a most important development of rail transport, and it gives promise of great extension in the future. The railways now are not merely carriers, but have become, in a sense, retail distributors. The new services are especially well adapted to modern trends in British trading methods, and they offer a means of meeting the competition of road transport in that form which has been most difficult to counteract, namely the private fleets of motor vehicles operated by manufacturers and distributors.

## CHAPTER XVI

## STATE OWNERSHIP OF RAILWAYS

FROM the earliest days of railways, and in every country, there has been a close contact between the railways and the State. This connexion may take several forms, which may be divided broadly into State Control and State Ownership. In no country has the State allowed full freedom to private enterprises in the management of their railways. On the contrary, a greater or less degree of State control has been exercised so that the railways might be regulated in the public interest.[1]

Though private ownership of railways, except for local lines, is confined to a minority of countries, the mileage under private ownership is more than 60 per cent. of the world's total railway mileage. In Great Britain, the United States, Spain, and Turkey the railways are entirely run by private enterprise, while in Argentina, Canada, Portugal, and Sweden a very large percentage is similarly owned and operated by companies.

Where a railway is State-owned it does not follow that it will necessarily be worked by the State. Just as under private enterprise a railway company may be leased by another company, so State-owned railways may be handed over to a company to be operated; e.g. in Holland, France, and India certain State-owned lines are worked by companies. In some countries the State, though it has not undertaken the responsibility of building railways, has aided their promotion by making free grants of land,

[1] See Chapter II.

e.g. in Canada, or has guaranteed interest on the bonds of private companies. In other countries the railways were built by private enterprise, but were later taken over by the State.

In view of the variations in the types of relationships between States and their railways it is necessary to distinguish carefully between *State Control, State Ownership,* and *State Operation.* State Control implies merely the regulation of railways neither owned nor operated by the State. State Ownership means that the State owns the railways and is responsible for finding the necessary capital, but it does not necessarily mean that the State operates the system. In State Operation is found the closest connexion between the State and a railway, since the system is both owned and operated by the State.[2]

The motives which have led Governments to nationalize their railways have been various. In backward or new countries the State has been forced to undertake construction, since private enterprise would not have been attracted. But not only have railways been regarded as an instrument of economic development; they have also been regarded as an instrument of political power, and many States have nationalized their railways for reasons of national defence or aggression. Administrative reasons, tariff customs policy, or the desire for national economic integration have also been factors. Thus railways have been built in Russia, Germany, and India for military, strategic, or administrative reasons; in Australia and the Union of South Africa in order to further economic development where private enterprise would not have been attracted; in Belgium and Switzerland in order that a national system of railways built to a regular plan might be provided, while in Canada the old ' Inter-Colonial Railway ' was constructed to connect Nova Scotia and New Brunswick with the rest of Canada for administrative or

---

[2] Municipal ownership and operation is also to be found in practice, e.g. the Nidd Valley Light Railway (now closed), but generally such lines are of the nature of tramways.

political purposes. In yet other countries railways have been nationalized with the idea of providing better services or lower charges than private enterprise was expected to give.

## STATE OWNERSHIP AND STATE OPERATION

In general, State railways are administered and operated by the State itself. The Railway Administration forms one of the Government Departments comparable to the Post Office in this country, and at its head is a Minister of the Political Party or Group in power at the time. Control is therefore of the political order, as the Minister is directly responsible to Parliament and must be prepared at any time to answer questions in Parliament about the conduct of the system. The permanent officials and staff are under the general control of the Minister, and their position is comparable to that of civil servants employed, for example, by the Post Office or Ministry of Transport. The railway budget, like the Post Office budget or the Road Fund in this country, is not kept separate from the general budget of the State, and therefore losses may be made good out of taxation or profits may be used for the general purposes of the State. The majority of the State railways are operated in this fashion, e.g. the Italian State Railways, the Swiss Federal Railways, and the State Railway in France.

## NEW TYPES OF STATE ADMINISTRATION

During recent years there has been a tendency to re-cast the relationship of State-owned railways to the Government. This is part of a general movement which appears slowly to be taking place in regard to the administrative character of State enterprise. In essentials the change has taken the form of setting up *ad hoc* bodies, or Boards, to control the special enterprises on behalf of the community, but without the day-to-day interference of Parliament. It

may be illustrated by the American demand to ' Take the
tariff out of Politics ', or the establishment of the Federal
Reserve Board to control Central Banking in the U.S.A.
In our own country the system goes back a long way,
as illustrated by the Acts setting up ' Trust Ports ' such
as the Port of London Authority or the Leith Dock Commission, but recently it has been considerably extended,
as witness the formation of the ' British Broadcasting
Corporation ' or the ' Central Electricity Board ' as
independent authorities with their own budgets separated
respectively from those of the Post Office and the Ministry
of Transport.

Experience has shown that the older type of State
administration had certain defects when applied to commercial or industrial undertakings. Briefly these were
the danger of undue political interference, routine methods,
or lack of continuity of policy. It was with the intention
of removing or diminishing the disadvantages while retaining State ownership and working that the new method of
administration has been adopted. The Railway Department with its political head and subject to the direct
interference of Parliament is replaced by a ' Commission '
or ' company ' organization. Control of general policy is
entrusted to a commission or board, the members of which
are appointed by Parliament for fixed periods of office
irrespective of changes in the fortunes of political parties.
The members are supposed to be appointed for their
experience of affairs, their special knowledge, or as
representatives of various interests, but not on the ground
of their political opinions. The General Manager, who is
responsible to the Board, is given a much freer hand and
more responsibility than the Permanent Secretary of the
ordinary Government department, so that he may operate
the system on commercial methods. He has only to
justify his policy before the Board and is not subject to
the restrictions imposed by having to provide adequate
answers in Parliament through his chief to any questions
put by Members, or to risk a reduction in the annual

parliamentary vote for his department. A further advantage is that the State does not become a party to labour disputes in the industry, and the political power of the large number of railwaymen and their dependents cannot be used as it might were railway questions to come directly before Parliament. Finally a most important difference is that the railway budget is separated from that of the State, and the railways are supposed to be worked so that they will pay their way as a commerical undertaking, neither giving nor receiving financial support. The Commission method has been adopted with considerable success by the Canadian National Railways where a Board has been established, representative of all interests concerned; by the German State Railway Company under the conditions of the Dawes Scheme of Reparations; and by the Belgian State Railway Company when the State railway was mortgaged as security for credits needed to effect currency stabilization. In Berlin an important merger of the various forms of city transport was effected in 1928 under municipal auspices, and the Berlin Transport Company thus established is controlled by a Commission.[3]

ADVANTAGES AND LIMITATIONS OF THE COMMISSION METHOD

The new method of State administration has obvious advantages over the old, since it strengthens the organization in those directions in which experience has shown that State railways are handicapped, e.g. lack of initiative, routine, and non-continuity of policy. Sir William Acworth, writing in 1920, strongly advocated the operation of State railways by independent boards. ' It is impossible ', he said, ' to obtain satisfactory results on Government railways in a democratic State unless the management is cut loose from direct political control. . . . Some day, perhaps, having learned wisdom by experience, a Parliament and a people may recognize that management for the people is not necessarily management by the

[3] See the author's *Transport Co-ordination*, pp. 119-22.

O

people; that there are other branches of government, besides the judicial branch, unsuited for popular interference '.

Opponents of nationalization say, however, that the commission method does not completely eliminate the political element, since appointments may be made to the board on political grounds and there is not the same spur to efficiency as exists in a profit-making enterprise. The board, they say, may become autocratic, and it is not subject to the same pressure of public opinion as other types of railway administration. Moreover, what the State gives the State can take away, and hence the commission may be more sensible to political pressure than private enterprise. Where the Board is composed of representatives of divergent interests, it may be difficult to secure the adoption of a consistent policy, and expensive developments which appeal to some of the members might be pushed through against the advice of the technicians.

### RAILWAY NATIONALIZATION

Much has been written on the question of Nationalization of Railways *versus* Private Enterprise, but opinions differ so widely that in a book of this nature it would seem best merely to set out the main factors which require to be taken into account in arriving at a decision. In the first place, care must be taken to distinguish between economic and other arguments in favour of State-ownership. Nationalization could be urged, for instance, on military or strategic grounds, but this would raise wider issues than the purely economic. Then in considering the purely economic arguments for, say, the nationalization of British railways, care must be taken not to credit advantages to nationalization which could also be obtained by reorganization under private enterprise if an economic case could be made out for them. Thus it is often asserted that nationalization would be advantageous on account of unity of management, amalgamation, extended ' common user ' of wagons, elimination of much of the work of the Railway

Clearing House, etc. But if these were considered desirable they could be obtained either by agreement or by compulsion, while retaining private enterprise, and in the past the railways have not shown any reluctance to combine if they were permitted to do so. The only possible argument in favour of nationalization under this head is that amalgamation would be more easily effected under State management, but this is of doubtful validity. Nor can it be argued that in general, State management is necessary to enable new developments to be undertaken, e.g. electrification. If the new methods were economically advantageous, presumably the railway companies in their own interests would adopt them just as readily as State management, though in certain circumstances the State may be able to look further ahead or to borrow money for improvements on more advantageous terms. Nor would the expenses of State control of private railways be wholly eliminated through nationalization. A Railway Commission would be required to adjust relations between a State railway and its customers just as much as in the case of private companies. In Prussia, for example, the Advisory Railway Councils were able to exert considerable pressure on the railway authorities, especially in regard to the grant of special (*ausnahme*) rates, and in 1906 about two-thirds of the goods traffic was carried at such rates, and there were nearly a thousand different rate-books in use.[4]

The case for nationalization has to be decided on broad issues and on the specific merits and limitations of private versus State enterprise. No doubt in different countries or at different times the weight which is to be attached to the individual arguments will vary to some extent, and the decision will be influenced by the actual conditions at the particular time. Briefly, the arguments in favour of nationalization may be summarized as follows:

(1) State railways have an advantage in the compulsory acquisition of lands, wayleaves, and easements, e.g. British

[4] Report. Board of Trade Conference. (Cd. 4677, 1909.)

O*

railways have had to pay far higher prices for their land than the State-constructed lines of the Continent.

(2) Developments and extensions which offer no immediate return, but which are likely to be beneficial in the more distant future, can be more readily undertaken by State railways, since the State can take a longer view than a private company, which has to earn dividends for its present shareholders. This argument applies with special force to new countries.

(3) Profits, if any, over and above interest rates would revert to the community in the form of lower charges and improved services or as contributions to the national exchequer.

(4) Railways are public utilities essential to the economic life of the nation and therefore ought to be community-owned and operated in the national interest.

(5) Conditions of service would be improved for the staff. Experience shows, however, that wages and conditions of service are sometimes better and sometimes worse under State management. The present conditions of railway servants in Great Britain compare favourably with those of certain State employees, and it is a well-known fact that the salaries of the higher grades of the Civil Service are lower than those paid in industry for similar positions of responsibility.

(6) Interest rates would be lower, since the State can generally borrow money on the most favourable terms because its security is greater. On the other hand, railways are also able to borrow on advantageous terms, though not at such low rates as the State. The fact that ordinary shares may receive little or no dividends must also be taken into account, since the State would have to meet fixed charges for interest whatever the conditions. In good times, however, the rate would not increase as might the dividends on ordinary shares.

(7) The State might be able to take a stronger line in regard to certain operating economies, e.g. elimination of private owners' wagons.

The arguments generally urged in favour of private enterprise and against railway nationalization are briefly as follows:

(1) It is said that experience shows that Government ownership and working is less efficient than private enterprise. The profit-making motive is said to act as a spur to innovations, to check waste and increase efficiency, whereas State management would be more costly and the numbers of the staff might be unduly increased.

(2) Since confiscation or partial confiscation would be both unjust and impracticable, railway bonds would have to be issued on which the interest charges would be equivalent or nearly equivalent to the dividends now paid. Therefore reduced cost in meeting capital charges would not be effected, though when new capital had to be raised the State might obtain it somewhat more cheaply than a private company.

(3) As against the argument for democratic control, it is urged that this would prove illusory and that sectional, not national, interests might be served. There might be undue political interference on behalf of favoured individuals or interests.

(4) While it might be easy to effect big, spectacular improvements which would attract the attention of the press and the public, it might be more difficult to obtain money for those smaller, inconspicuous, day-to-day improvements which would probably produce, in the end, greater public benefit. For example, the Central Electricity Board launched out on a very extensive programme of general electrical distribution, but the ' grid ' is said to be seriously underloaded owing to the lack of demand, and therefore costs cannot be reduced.

(5) The desire to safeguard national property might lead to the imposition of unfair burdens on other forms of transport, though on the other hand the State might be able to introduce a larger measure of compulsory co-ordination than is possible under private enterprise.

This last consideration has been important in the

proposal for the setting up of a Transport Board for passenger transport in London. Co-ordination between the motor-buses, trams, and tubes is very desirable, and it has seemed that the best method of achieving this would be to set up a public trust or board, independent of political or municipal parties, which would provide a common management for all the forms of local transport, and pool their financial resources. In order to achieve complete co-ordination it has been agreed that the receipts from suburban lines belonging to the main line railways should be included in the pool, which would be divided out as between the Board and the railways in proportion to their ascertained receipts from such traffic during an agreed standard year. The scheme also envisages the setting up of a joint committee for the discussion of such matters as through running, interavailability of tickets, through booking, etc.

It is generally agreed that the formation of a London Passenger Transport Board, which in effect means community ownership of the trams, buses, and tubes, is desirable, but there is no such unanimity of opinion regarding the nationalization of the whole railway system. Readers therefore must be left to form their own conclusions on this wide problem of railway economics.

## CHAPTER XVII

# THE PRESENT POSITION AND FUTURE PROSPECTS OF BRITISH RAILWAYS

SINCE the war the growth of road transport and the continued depression in the basic industries of the country have had serious reactions on the financial prosperity of the railways. Railway revenues have fallen off, but it has not been possible to effect a proportionate reduction in expenditure because by its very nature a railway is burdened with a large proportion of fixed costs. The railways, moreover, whatever may be the position in regard to other types of transport, have to meet without subsidy of any kind all the expenses, both capital and annual, involved in providing and working their road, signalling, stations, and rolling stock.

The railways were slow to realize the seriousness of road competition, and it was only in 1928 that they made a determined and successful attempt to obtain general road powers. They are now in a better position to co-ordinate road and rail services, though they are still hindered in their competition with road hauliers by various legal restrictions, especially those relating to undue preference, which do not apply to transport by road. Some modification of these legal burdens would seem to be desirable under modern conditions, as they bear heavily on the railways, though they may have been necessary in the days when railways had a practical monopoly of inland transport.

At the time of writing, with traffic still continuing to fall off and road transport competition still unabated, the financial prospects for the railways are far from bright. On the other side of the picture, however, it is to be remembered that since 1921 the railways have effected great economies in working costs; they have introduced many new technical improvements; and the managements have shown an increasing alertness to try out new methods. If trade were to revive, the railways would be in a far stronger position than they are to-day, since the law of decreasing costs might be expected to operate.

As regards the trend of developments in the near future, it would appear that electrification will be favoured for the more important suburban lines, but not for main line working. The steam locomotive in all probability will be further improved, but it may have to meet keen competition from its new rival in the form of the oil-electric locomotive. There would seem to be great possibilities in the development of signalling methods, and it may confidentially be expected that much will be done in this direction. It is also possible that the adoption of continuous brakes for all trains may be favoured, as this would enable many of the advantages of electric traction to be obtained at less cost than that required to provide electric equipment. The main obstacles to achieving this important improvement are the difficulties and expense of shunting and marshalling braked trains. Standardization and economies in the workshops are likely to increase. In most departments there will probably be a marked tendency to adopt labour-saving devices on as large a scale as possible, and indeed this would appear to be necessary if wage rates are to be maintained.

In administration the tendency would seem to be towards the adoption of a modified divisional type of organization. In connexion with road transport competition and the operation of co-ordinated road-rail services, this is desirable, and it would become essential if further amalgamation were effected. Further combination, indeed, seems to be foreshadowed, though this may not necessarily take the form of complete amalgamation, since many of the economies could be obtained by means of traffic pools and the readjustment of the ownership of certain lines.

An important development is also suggested by the tentative alterations which have recently been made towards the simplification of the complicated classifications and tariffs for rates and fares. It is impossible to say how far this movement will be carried, as much will depend on the success obtained from experimental alterations.

The railway system still forms the backbone of the transport facilities of Great Britain, and for many kinds of traffic the rail is still supreme. In the future, however, it will be necessary to increase co-ordination among the various forms of transport so that the community may receive the best possible service at the least cost. Co-ordination presents the only basis for the elimination of wasteful competition and therefore it is essential that all the possibilities should be fully explored. More branch lines and intermediate stations will probably have to be closed, but main line and important cross-country services should be improved and accelerated. In general, local transport, except that of a very intensive character, is most suitable to the road, but medium and long-distance traffic should be attracted to the rail. If co-ordination were effected on a large scale, the railway stations would become great distribution centres for all kinds of road and rail traffic, and from these focal points road, rail, and even air transport services would radiate in all directions.

# SELECT BIBLIOGRAPHY

THE following list of books does not pretend to be a complete bibliography of railway literature, which has now grown to be very extensive. The author has based his selection on the principle of mentioning all works which he has found of special value in the compilation of the present volume and which may prove useful to the student of railway economics. As a guide to readers who may desire to form a small railway library of their own, suitable and for the most part less expensive works are marked with an asterisk.

## GENERAL

\*SIR WILLIAM ACWORTH and W. T. STEPHENSON. *Elements of Railway Economics.* 1924.

\*E. CLEVELAND-STEVENS. *English Railways: Their Development and their Relation to the State.* 1915.

K. G. FENELON. *Transport and Communications.* 1931.

A. T. HADLEY. *Railroad Transportation.* 1897.

E. JONES. *Principles of Railway Transportation.* 1925.

\*A. W. KIRKALDY and A. EVANS. *History and Economics of Transport.* 1924.

D. KNOOP. *Outlines of Railway Economics.* 1925.

D. LARDNER. *Railway Economy.* 1850.

A. MARSHALL. *Industry and Trade.* 1919.

LORD MONKSWELL. *Railways of Great Britain.* 1926.

E. PROTHEROE. *Railways of the World.* (Undated, about 1912.)

W. Z. RIPLEY. *Railroads.* 1927. Vol. I, *Rates and Regulations.* Vol. II, *Finance and Organization.*

\*C. E. R. SHERRINGTON. *Economics of Rail Transport in Great Britain.* 1928. Vol. I, *History and Development.* Vol. II, *Rates and Service.*

\*W. V. WOOD and SIR JOSIAH STAMP. *Railways.* 1928.

*Modern Railway Administration.* 2 vols. 1925.

JOHNSON, HUEBNER, and WILSON. *Principles of Transportation.* (New York.) 1928.

218

## RAILWAY DEVELOPMENT

W. M. Acworth. *Railways and the Traders.* 1891.
R. Bell. *A Hundred Years of Railway Development.* (Journal, Institute of Transport. 1928. Vol. VII, pp. 177-88.)
J. H. Clapham. *Economic Development of France and Germany.* 1921.
*L. Knowles. *Industrial and Commercial Revolutions in Great Britain.* 1921.
W. T. Jackman. *Transportation in Modern England.* 2 vols. 1916.
H. G. Lewin. *Early History of British Railways.* 1925.
*E. A. Pratt. *History of Transport and Communications in England.* 1912.

## REGULATION OF RAILWAYS BY THE STATE

*H. Barr Davies. *The Rights and Duties of Transport Undertakings.* 1926.
H. W. Disney. *The Law of Carriage by Railway.* 1923.
J. Fergusson. *Public Statutes relating to Railways in Scotland.* 1898.
J. D. I. Hughes. *Law of Transport by Rail.* 1931.
J. S. Jeans. *Railway Problems.* 1887.
E. R. Johnson. *American Railway Transportation.* 1910.
A. Leslie. *Law of Transport by Railway.*
L. R. Lipsett and T. J. D. Atkinson. *Law of Carriage by Railway in Great Britain and Ireland.*

## RAILWAY ORGANIZATION

*T. B. Hare. *British Railway Operating.* 1927.
*D. R. Lamb. *Modern Railway Operation.* 1926.
Travis, Lamb, and Jenkinson. *Practical Railway Working.* 1915.
H. M. Hallsworth. *Elements of Railway Operating.* (Out of print.)
P. H. Price. *The Railway Clearing House.* (Journal, Institute of Transport. 1926. Vol. VII, pp. 329-42.)
R. Morris. *Railroad Administration.* 1930.

## RAILWAY LABOUR

R. Bell. *Education and Training for Railway Work.* (Paper read at Meeting of Great Central Railway Debating Society, Nottingham.) 1928.

*K. J. N. Browne. *Brown and Other Systems of Railway Discipline.* 1923.
J. Cunnison. *Labour Organization.* 1930.
J. W. F. Rowe. *Wages in Theory and Practice.* 1928.
S. and B. Webb. *History of Trade Unionism.* 1920.
G. D. H. Cole and P. Arnot. *Trade Unionism on the Railways.*
H. Blake and W. Jackson. *Electric Railway Transportation.* (New York.) 1917. Chaps. XV-XIX.

## RAILWAY AMALGAMATION

*W. A. Robertson. *Combination among Railway Companies.* 1912.
*Sir Josiah Stamp. *Industrial and Railway Amalgamations.*

## THE RAILWAYS ACT 1921

Sir William Acworth. *Grouping under the Railways Act, 1921.* (Economic Journal. 1923. Vol. XXXIII, p. 19.)
Aggs and Knowles. *Handbook on Railways.* 1922.
R. P. Griffiths. *The Railways Act, 1921.* 1925.
G. Garro Jones. *Railway Rates Tribunal; Jurisdiction and Practice.* 1923.
H. C. Kidd. *A New Era for British Railways.* 1929.
J. W. Parker. *Traders' Rail Charges Up-to-date.* 1928.
W. E. Simnett. *Railway Amalgamations in Great Britain.* 1923.
*Annual Reports of the Railway Rates Tribunal.*

## RATES AND FARES

J. M. Clark. *Economics of Overhead Costs.* 1923.
C. Colson. *Cours D'Économie Politique.* (Livre Sixième.) 1910.
C. Colson. *Railway Rates and Traffic.* (Translated C. Travis.) 1914.
*H. G. Brown. *Transportation Rates and their Regulation.* 1921.
*P. Burtt. *Railway Rates: Principles and Problems.* 1926.
E. R. Johnson and G. G. Huebner. *Railroad Traffic and Rates.*
*H. Marriott. *Fixing of Rates and Fares.* 1908.
E. A. Pratt. *Railways and their Rates.* 1905.
S. J. McLean. *Inland Traffic.* 1919. (Describes Canadian Rate Structure.)
*Statutory Rules and Orders.* 1927. No. 850. Railway Schedule of Standard Charges.

## ELECTRIFICATION

P. BURTT. *Railway Electrification and Traffic Problems.*
1929.
*\*Report of Committee on Main Line Electrification.* 1931.
J. P. THOMAS. *Handling London's Underground Traffic.*
1928.
A. T. DOVER. *Electric Traction.* 1919.
H. F. TREWMAN. *Railway Electrification.* 1924.

## ROAD TRANSPORT SERVICES

\*K. G. FENELON. *Transport Co-ordination.* 1929.
K. G. FENELON. *Economics of Road Transport.* 1925.
K. G. FENELON. *Road Transport Costs.* (Accountants'
Magazine, August, 1930.)
H. M. McLEAN. *Motor Transport Costs and Charges.*
(Sydney.) 1931.
J. PHILLIMORE. *Motor Road Transport.* (Undated.)

## ECONOMICS OF TRAIN WORKING

CECIL J. ALLEN. *Railways of To-day.*
T. B. HARE. *Practical Railway Operating.* 1931.
*\*Final Report of the Royal Commission on Transport.* 1931.
*\*Report of the Royal Commission on the Coal Industry.*
1926. Cmd. 2600.
*Report of Standing Committee on Mineral Transport.* 1931.
Cmd. 3751.
P. BURTT. *Principal Factors in Freight Train Operating.*
1923.
E. R. B. ROBERTS. *British Railways and Unemployment.*
1931.

## STATE OWNERSHIP

\*W. M. ACWORTH. *State Railway Ownership.* 1920.
A. E. DAVIES. *Why Nationalization is Inevitable.* 1924.
CLEMENT EDWARDS. *Railway Nationalization.* 1898.
H. M. JAGTIANI. *The Rôle of the State in the Provision
of Railways.* 1924.
E. A. PRATT. *Railways and Nationalization.* 1911.
W. M. W. SPLAWN. *Government Ownership and Operation
of Railroads.* 1928.
A. G. WALKDEN. *A Practical Scheme for the Nationaliza-
tion and Co-ordination of Public Transport.* 1931.
*The State in Relation to Railways.* (Royal Economic
Society.) 1912.

## ACCOUNTS AND STATISTICS

A. E. KIRKUS. *Railway Statistics: Their Compilation and Use.* 1927.

C. P. MOSSOP. *Railway Operating Statistics.* 1923.

C. H. NEWTON. *Railway Accounts.* 1930.

*Ministry of Transport.* Annual Railway Returns.

## JOURNALS AND PERIODICALS

*Journal of the Institute of Transport.*
*Railway Gazette.*
*Modern Transport.*
*Railway Age* (American).
*Railway Review.*
*Railway Newsletter.*
*The World's Carriers.*
*The Electric Railway, Bus, and Tram Journal.*
*L.N.E.R. Magazine.*
*L.M.S.R. Magazine.*
*Transport Management.*
*Tramway and Railway World.*
*Times Trade Supplement.*
*Manchester Guardian Commercial.*

# INDEX